Endorsements for Ed

God knew what He was doing when He :
in marriage. Mixing the two of us togetl
for both of us. My finding God without th
in the church before finding God produced curiosity and revelation. As a Registered Counsellor, I have an understanding of how we are whole beings created with body, spirit, and soul, being our mind, will, and emotions. Nothing happens to one part without affecting all other parts of us. Therefore, it is necessary to see ourselves from the original design that God created us with. Understanding and care need to be holistic. Research is proving what God has always known, that compassion for self is healing. There is a reason He tells us to love others as Christ has loved us. We are to understand how He loves us and love ourselves that way. This helps us then love others the same way. As a world, we need this desperately. This book provides insight into a needed revelation of God's love and design for His creation.

These pages contain an understanding of Matt's journey from law to love. I have had the privilege of being a part of this journey since 1990 when we got married, but his story started long before that. The mixture of our two personalities has been quite a ride. We have journeyed through some extremely difficult relationship choices and experiences together. However, none of it has been wasted. Everything we endured and overcame together became the soil for a seed of love to die in so the seedling of love could grow.

Matt has travelled through valleys and up mountains with God in both the physical and the spiritual planes. He has searched his own heart and God's heart to find connection and freedom. Through getting curious, asking questions and humbly accepting direction from God, Matt's understanding of love has shifted so far away from right and wrong which led to shame, toward unending grace which produced life.

His understanding of Eden as the place of God's blueprint of creation was increased by a revelation of love that began in the unlikely place of the slums of Beirut, Lebanon, where he looked through the lens of all-encompassing love to better grasp his beliefs. This book contains the beginning of his journey to greater love for God, self and everyone else.

His revelation of the Two Trees in Eden gives a scaffold for how to understand our own view of God and how He views us. We do not have to strive, but live free, abundant lives. Nothing is withheld from us. All we need to do is love God with all our heart, soul, and strength, and learn to love ourselves as He loves us which will make us perfect lovers of everyone else. This is our invitation.

These pages drip with the honey of love and grace that has flowed from the Father to Matt. There is no judgment, but there has been raw exploration to work out his path toward a greater revelation of love. Enjoy the adventure.

Trish Beckenham
Registered Counsellor and Co-Founder, Greater Things International
www.greaterthingsinternational.com

One of the blessings of this book is listening to Matt's expectations of God. They are expectations soaked in God's presence with us. At every turn in this book, I felt God present with me. It is more than the words. It is the profound realisation that God is present with me and his heart is always for me. A truly beautiful read, and one where I forgot completely that I was reading and simply entered into the presence of God.

Michael James Henderson
Artist & Writer
www.michaeljameshenderson.com.au

From the moment I started reading the introduction of Matt's book, *Eden's Blueprint*, I felt everything around me grow slow and still. Every truth that Matt pens awakened something in my heart, and made me feel a sense of great hunger for deeper intimacy with the Heavenly Father and with others. Matt's vulnerability is refreshing as he exposes shame's deceptive nature, and smashes its influence over children of God. His ability to invite the human heart into the very rhythm of the Father's heartbeat for ourselves and others is powerful, and his revelation on our restoration back to the image of God carries a breakthrough anointing. As a personal friend, I know that Matt lives what he writes, and I am so grateful that he is releasing this revelation and impartation to the world through this book.

Mandy Woodhouse
Founder, Mandy Woodhouse - Outrageous Hope
www.mandywoodhouseoutrageoushope.com
Speaker and author, #Free_Indeed and Daughter in the Meadow

For many years Matt Beckenham has sought the heart of the Father for the Bride of Christ. In this book, *Eden's Blueprint*, Matt beautifully encourages, challenges, and expands our understanding of the Kingdom of God, both on Earth and within our relationships. *Eden's Blueprint* comes from deep within the place of study and intimate relationship with the Father, Son, and Holy Spirit over many years and through the challenges of various seasons of life. This book profoundly details what happens when we embrace our relationship with God and begin to understand the beauty of our design; we return home to Him and ourselves.

Courtney Kueck
www.greaterthingsinternational.com
www.facebook.com/courtney.kueck

Matt Beckenham is someone you walk away from a conversation feeling like you have just drunk from the most refreshing streams of living water. He speaks truth with a father's heart and a heart full of God's love. His words carry revelation and freedom. I know this book will be one that will give people permission to breathe again, dream again, and really know the depth of the Father's love for them. This is a book that can be read time and time again and carry fresh revelation each time.

Lisa Bruton
Director and founder of Arise Sanctuary
www.lisabruton.com.au

My friend Matt Beckenham's book *Eden's Blueprint* is a deep well of encounter with the love of God. As you read its pages you will be saturated in God's heart for you as His son, His daughter to live in deep relationship with Jesus, free from shame, living in deeper depths of freedom, deeply awakened to your identity in Christ and burning with the revelation of His ferocious love towards you. This book is a blazing trumpet, heralding an invitation into a deeper revelation of our original design. A deeper place of intimacy with our Beloved and His Words of love and truth are awaiting you in this beautiful book.

Lana Vawser
Founder, Lana Vawser Ministries
www.lanavawser.com

There's something so tangible about the love of the Father that flows through my friend, Matt Beckenham. It seems in some ways beyond understanding, somewhat unexplainable yet at the same time deeper than the deepest well and wider than the most magnificent horizon.

Spending time with Matt is like spending time with the Father. That's what you'll find as you open the pages of *Eden's Blueprint* and let the words invade the spaces of your heart where you've wondered what the love of the Lord is really, truly like.

Matt has this beautiful way of releasing truth and revelation — he wraps it in love and original design, and it then sparks and ignites your innermost being, bringing to the surface the gold from within that's been waiting, longing, yearning to see the light.

Know that you're going to come alive more than you ever have. You're going to encounter new thought spaces to think thoughts that you've never thought before. And, you will have ah-ha moments that will blow your mind. Come, my friend, into the pages of Matt's journey with awe and wonder and be met by the enduring love of our good, good Father.

Kerri-Ann Luketic
Brilliance Coach, Kingdom Thought Technician, Author,
Prophetic Artist
www.kerriannluketic.com.au

In Paul's letter to Philemon, the apostle describes this church leader as someone who has a 'love toward the Lord Jesus and all the saints.' He also describes him as someone who 'refreshes the saints' – this beautiful description can be as easily applied to Matt and all that he does for the Kingdom, and *Eden's Blueprint* is no exception. But I would go further to say that this book will not only refresh the saints but will also challenge, change, save and release many into freedom!

The vulnerability required to write a book like this needs not only bravery but a security in the Father, both of which I know Matt has, and helps others to have too.

Sometimes you read a book that so resonates with your heart you can breathe a huge sigh of relief in the knowledge that the revelations you have been receiving are being experienced by others – I cannot think of anyone better than Matt to be able to share these Kingdom discoveries with the world – and he does so in such a beautiful, honesty and readable way.

May you be blessed as you read of the love that bears, believes, hopes and trusts all things, and may you experience and encounter that love, from the Father who loves you!

Rev'd Carl Smith
Church of England Vicar and Writer, UK

Eden's Blueprint is a refreshing and timely read for anyone that's sick and tired of running the religious treadmill. Matt will take you on an adventure back to the Garden of Eden, where he captures the Father's heart and design for all of His creation – especially His Sons and Daughters. It's through this design and intentional purpose, that Matt unpacks the invitation of identity, purpose and freedom the Father longs to give to all those who would receive His gift. This book exposes the mundane, effort and obligation of religion to discover and release the provision, restoration and empowering of the Father for all who accept His invitation. Do yourself a favour and step beyond the status quo of expectation and revisit and rediscover a life that's worth living from the design of *Eden's Blueprint*.

Rob Feeney
Senior Leader, Gracepoint Christian Church
www.gracepoint.com.au

EDEN'S
BLUEPRINT

EDEN'S BLUEPRINT

God's Plan for Your Life
Began with a Design

MATT BECKENHAM

TRULY LOVED MEDIA
JER 31:3

trulyloved.media

ISBN: 979-8-9853467-2-5 (Paperback)

ISBN: 979-8-9853467-3-2 (Hardcover)

Cover Design: Michelle Mauricio

Published by

Truly Loved Media
7643 Gate Pkwy, Ste 104-374
Jacksonville, FL 32256

www.trulyloved.media

DEDICATION

For Trish, my wife, and closest friend.

*Without you, none of this would have been possible
and I'd still be sitting under the wrong tree.*

CONTENTS

FOREWORD

by Lana Vawser

Eden's Blueprint is a blazing trumpet, heralding an invitation into deeper revelation of our original design. It is an invitation into deeper realms of intimacy with Jesus, freedom in Him and an awakening of identity. We have entered a new era, and I believe the Lord is doing many wonderful and glorious things. His movement through the chambers toward His bride is breathtaking. He is bringing forth an alignment, awakening and a wooing to return to our first love, our beautiful Jesus who is leading us into the realms of freedom and revelation of identity that He paid for us to walk in. There is a depth of intimacy and a lingering communion with the Lord that He is inviting us into in this new era, a place that we have not walked in before. It is a deep place where freedom, healing, deliverance and a thriving in who we are in Christ is coming forth. As we listen to His heart, as we come completely undone by the ferocious love of Christ and the pure burning love of the Father, we are brought back into the revelation of our original design.

It's a place where the truth of His Word, the relentless love of the Father, the voice of Holy Spirit is breaking off the stifling lids and limitations that have long held us down and kept us contained. These limitations were not part of our original design and God's original intent for us to walk in. His glory is matchless, His freedom is unlimited. There is a simplifying that is taking place as we walk with Him. There is a simplicity and a depth all at the same time that the Spirit of God is ushering us into as we walk with Him in the Garden.

There is a mighty detoxification taking place amongst His people and disillusionment is falling. Things that we have carried and boxes we have been put in or told we must stay in by people, or the world's system or lies of the enemy, are now breaking. The Lord is raising up a people who know they were born to shine His light. They know they were born not to fit in, but to stand out. Set apart. Holy. Consecrated.

They were born to know love, to be in relationship with the most perfect form of love, God Himself, and to be love in the earth. To be the very hands and feet of Jesus. To carry His heart. To look for Him everywhere. To authentically love the one before them because they live in and from a place of being totally undone and overcome by the ferocious love of the Father. A father who sent His Son Jesus, who laid down His life for them to not only be reconciled to Him and to spend eternity with Him, but also to remove the hold of things that come to hinder relationship with Him. Shame no longer has a voice. Condemnation no longer has a voice. Heaviness and guilt no longer have a voice, because LOVE made a way. Christ made a way. His voice speaks a better word over you. As we walk with Him in the quiet of the Garden, we hear His voice, the voice that calls us to life. It brings us to life. The words that flow from His heart and His love awaken us. The voice that reminds us who we are. The encounters and experiences with the eyes of Jesus that burn like flames of fire, transform us and that love now flows through us and brings transformation to the world around us. We live in this beautiful Garden place, the Eden place, deep in His heart with unhindered access because of what Jesus paid for and it changes everything. My dear friend Matt Beckenham's book, *Eden's Blueprint*, has tapped the artesian well of the purity of this love. It will draw you into a deep encounter with the love of the Father and His relentless pursuit of you. As you sit in the places revealed in these pages, your heart will be marked afresh.

Matt holds such tenderness in his heart toward the Lord, the way he carries the Father's heart and the love of Christ pours out of Matt's heart and drips like oil over these pages. This book is a deep well that will refresh you. It is also a launching pad that will catapult you into deeper realms of transformation, healing, deliverance, awakening and revelation. As you read the words of Matt's life, may you hear the trumpet that is announcing a new day of freedom for you to walk in your original design in depths you've never walked in before. Acts 17:28 (NIV) says, "In Him we live and move and have our being."

As I read through these pages, I was deeply impacted by the wonderful reality that we have unhindered access to His heart and we live in Him, we move in Him, we breathe in Him, He surrounds us, He loves us, in Him we find life and it is His desire for us to know Him and His heart in unprecedented ways in this new era. There are glorious blueprints that God is releasing right now. Blueprints of strategy, new assignments, wisdom and intel from heaven. How wonderful it is to partner with Him in ALL He is doing and going to do in the earth. But it all must flow from the most glorious blueprint of all, walking with

Him in the Garden. The deep place of intimacy and communion with Him. The unhindered access to His heart. Friendship with God and ministering unto Him. From here, all else flows. It is my great honour, joy and privilege to recommend this profoundly deep and moving book that is an incredible gift to the global church, to you.

Lana Vawser
Founder, Lana Vawser Ministries
www.lanavawser.com

ACKNOWLEDGEMENTS

There have been so many that have helped me in this journey of publishing my very first book! Some have helped so powerfully in the revelation that I've attempted to articulate in these pages. There are many who have cheered me on from the sidelines.

Michelle Mauricio, thank you for your patience in editing and getting this whole thing to be published. Your creativity and expertise have gone beyond what I could have imagined.

Lisa & Mat Bruton, thank you for your generosity and belief in me. I'll be forever thankful that you have invested in this book.

Trish Beckenham and Erica Harris, thank you for the time you gave in the editing process and for giving me such wonderful feedback.

Thank you, Steve Frost, for introducing me to grace and saying the words, "I can help you." You are the one that carried the wooden sword for me and stood by me when few others would dare.

Thank you, Lana Vawser, for prophecying this book into being and for writing the foreword! It's been such a journey to get here, with much "stretching" along the way. Looking forward to all that God does through us in the years to come.

Thank you to Alia Abboud and the team at LSESD in Lebanon. You showed me a love that has forever changed me.

Thank you, Jessie DeCorsey, for taking the photos and helping us find the perfect Eden spot to take them.

Lastly, thank you to all who call me "friend." Your love has changed my life for the better, and made God a whole lot clearer for me.

PROLOGUE

Jesus would often teach about the Kingdom of God using parables, which are short stories/allegories of fiction that would help the listener gain a greater understanding or revelation. The opening and closing chapters of this book are similar. My prayer is that this will help you with the writings and revelations that are contained within all the other chapters.

My favourite time of day is the dawn; although most eagles wait until the heat of the day truly settles in before unfurling, I'm not like most eagles for I love the quiet that blankets the Garden just before the sun stretches itself out from side to side. I revel in watching as the Garden shimmers and awakens in the glorious light of its touch and I am filled with delight when the melodies of the day begin to rise, the fragrance of creatures moving in perfect harmony whispers through the treetops where I sit.

This is my home, this place where I take in the span of the Kingdom day after day as I breathe in the marvel of perfect design. I rest here in the peace of how I was designed, with precision and purpose, to be His eyes and ears and to report back to Him everything I see happening in the Garden, His Garden, the beloved blueprint of the *Designer* Himself.

I cannot wrestle with pride or doubt. These things are not a part of my design; it is honour and love that move my lens day after day. My cherished charges are the ones who look like Him. They move and breathe like Him too, and He entrusted them to me—the one called man and the other called woman—they are the ones whom all His love is poured out upon and I will shelter them with my majestic wings for all of my days.

I was there when His loving words flowed like honey into the man. He spoke to him about the fruit of the Garden, about the trees. He invited the man to cast his eyes over the Garden, to allow his senses to be awakened to the goodness of His provision, The man's eyes widened in wonder and gratitude. Awe covered him in beauty and he shimmered with love; he would lack nothing.

Then He invited the man to move his eyes to look upon the one tree that he was not invited to eat from. The tree was called *The Knowledge of Good and Evil* and every creature in the Garden knew that this tree was not designed for them. His honeyed words burnt with Holy fire when He spoke of this tree to the man and the man understood the weight of these words for they were written upon the man's heart.

And truly I tell you, the man lacked nothing, but more than that, he was given *everything*. As they spoke, I could see the trees responding to their conversation; they began to dance as the Designer's words brought refreshing to their limbs. He spoke of the tree called the *Tree of Life* and even as He spoke of His master creation he maintained no ownership over it but freely lavished it upon those in the Garden and upon the man, His *beloved* one.

The *Tree of Life* is the center of the blueprint. Every creature knows how life-giving that one tree truly is! You can see it, sense it: from it all things flow and move, all things are covered and unearthed beneath it, rivers flow from it and through it, oil and fire are breathed from its core and the fruit that it holds is beyond comprehension and yet makes perfect sense.

That was, until one of those days, in one of those weeks, in one of those months, in one of those years when *everything* changed.

Each day that rose in the Garden was another gift, another glimpse into the life running through that tree. I delighted in watching the man and then the woman feast on the most treasured fruits. I feasted myself, and as I did, a warmth flowed through me and out of me, and each cell within me came under the love that cascaded down as the fruit dripped and flowed through me. You see, I know the taste, I know the pleasure and day after day, week after week, month after month, and year after year, it was I who watched the man and the woman and every living thing partake in the most pure form of love ever known.

I knew them like I knew myself. I watched every path they would take and I was filled with joy looking upon them living in their perfect design, just as they were destined to. But the day that everything changed came swiftly, and I could not stop it, or save them, and I could not step outside of time and pull them back on track. It was their tracks that first concerned me: over time, their path began to widen, then move around differently. Their footsteps moved closer and closer to the tree that had not been offered to them.

Each day they would walk by. I flew closer when they did, but I didn't intervene; I just observed. One day I saw them point at the tree and then continue on. The next day they stopped at the tree and they spoke about it, wondering what the fruit might taste like, but they continued on their path and walked on by. I felt my feathers bristle, a sensation that had never occurred before. Until now, no creature had gone near the tree for we all knew the words spoken to the man and we all knew what would happen if the man and the woman ate from that tree.

During this time I saw something strange begin to happen. Each time the man and woman walked near the tree, all the creatures in the Garden became restless. The peace that the creatures walked in would start to splinter and bristle, and sometimes a mist would arise as confused murmurs began simmering. It only happened when the man and woman neared the tree, and as they moved away things would settle and again be as they were meant to be.

There are some days that remain etched in the mind, this was such a day. One of the animals in the Garden that the man had called a lizard wasn't acting like a lizard; it wasn't making lizard words and all the other lizards began avoiding it. I watched as the strange lizard began lurking near the *Tree of Knowledge of Good and Evil*, as though his steps were intentional, as though he was hunting for something. He began moving through the Garden differently. He steered clear of the *Tree of Life* and alarm rustled through me as he settled himself beneath the other tree. It was almost as if the atmosphere shifted; the Garden became still and moved in slow motion before my very eyes.

The woman called Eve walked the path alone that day and came upon the tree. The lizard appeared to be hoping in this, relying on this separation of the man and the woman, when suddenly out of its mouth came words like those that only the man and woman had spoken. I saw the sky grow dark and knew I had to move quickly! I had to tell the Designer—He needed to know what was happening under this tree!

But before I could take flight to find Him, I became acutely aware of His presence, as I realised He was sitting beside me in my watchtower tree. *He* was watching as well. My entire being was swirling with unease. I implored Him,

"My Lord, allow me to use the razor sharp talons you gave me: I will pluck that lizard away from the woman and drop him off a cliff ending this corruption!"

Gently He spoke to me,

"This is Eve's moment. She has been here before; she knows my words and now she has a choice."

Never before had I raised my voice to the Mighty One, but shrillness screamed out of me as I screeched,

"This will affect us all!"

All He said back to me was again,

"This is Eve's moment."

Aghast, I pleaded with Him,

"Allow me to bring the man, Adam, here. Surely he will stop this!"

"No," said my Lord, "I have given Adam my words. He knows them, and today we will see if he trusts them."

The Designer, my Lord, God of the universe, then turned toward me and, looking right into my being, said,

"Can you see what is happening to my creation when my words are silenced? Can you feel it in the air, and in the atmosphere? Can you see the turmoil within the animals? Can you feel it within yourself? You've never felt the feelings that are flowing through you right now, at this moment."

Every fiber of my being lurched and spilled out, and as tears began to sear my feathers, I cried,

"All this is wasted then, all of it... the peace, the harmony, the connection and the love."

"No," He replied, "nothing is wasted, the worst that this strange lizard can do is *nothing* compared to what my love can do. You are about to see the power of death in all of its fullness, but through it and given time, you will see the infinite power of my love. It is beyond anything and everything that a corrupt lizard can offer."

I sat next to my Lord, my Father, and watched in horror as Eve took a bite of the fruit, a trickle of crimson ran down her lips and chin. I grieved as I watched Adam move toward them and as Eve had eaten, so too did Adam. The strange lizard's face became distorted by a smug expression in the grave moment that the man Adam and the woman Eve realised exactly what they had done.

The lizard cackled and mocked, his laughter over their shame burning their skin, as they scrambled for leaves to cover themselves and tried to find a place to hide from God. The lizard had tried to hide from God once before but he quickly found out that there was *nowhere* he could hide. So that's what he did, that strange, distorted lizard. He just waited for God to come. And I could see into his soul; when God did come, the lizard in all of his filth would gloat.

The rage tore through me then. It was something I'd never felt before, and its power gripped me and terrified me. It almost lifted me away from myself when God's voice, the voice that soothes and heals, the voice that breathes life and cascades over grief like honey, gently settled me as He said,

"They have eaten the fruit that they were told not to, but there is the *Tree of Life* and it is not broken; it will continue to do all that I planned for it to do. If the strange lizard was wise, he would have tried to convince Adam and Eve that it should be chopped down, or destroyed. But he did not and he will soon see the error of his thinking."

Perching myself again, settling my wings, even in my nearness to the Holy of Holies I could not help but lament over all that I had just witnessed. A feeling of helplessness and uselessness came upon me, for

God had given me a job to watch over the ones like Him, the ones made in His image, His beloved Adam and Eve, and when all I wanted to do was protect them, rescue them, and prevent them from the gravest decision of their lives, the Mighty One had not allowed it. It was here that I first knew the wrestle of pride and doubt, and it was here that God reached out. He knew my thoughts, and He gently placed His hand upon my head and stroked it for a time, and as I had when He first created me, I relaxed beneath His touch, His love drawing me back to warmth and wholeness. Then He spoke out the words that shifted the atmosphere again and brought me to my knees with their beauty.

"You have been given the privilege of watching two of the most powerful forces that exist at work. The first is choice: the ability to choose to be in relationship with me. The second is love. When I get down from this tree and go and find my beloved ones, you will see the beginnings of the greatest love story that has ever been known, and this time, no strange lizard will be able to stop it."

God looked up at the sky and saw that the sun was setting, the warmth of the day was lifting, the stars would soon fill the sky with their glittering melodies as the cool of the evening moved through the Garden. I knew this was the time of day that God loved the most, it was the time when he would walk in the quiet of the evening with those He created to be in relationship with.

INTRODUCTION

I feel the timing of releasing this book is appropriate. The chaos in the world today has served to cause us as Christians to dig deeper into God. This is the beginning of my deeper journey revelations from being curious, asking questions, and seeking answers from The Father. I hope you will receive encouragement, revelation, and understanding of the incredible love that God has for us all as you read it.

I've called it *Eden's Blueprint*. To me, the Garden of Eden represents God's heart. Eden has occasionally been treated as mythical. However, I believe that through Jesus' life, death, and resurrection, God has re-opened Eden for us all to return to our original design.

In my journey, I had become frustrated with religion and began believing for more. Theologies seemed to make God so complicated that understanding Him was out of reach for most. I was being told "there is more," but not being helped to understand the more I was promised. I was frustrated with metaphors that seemed to describe something fantastical but had no application to me tangibly. So I started searching. I started deconstructing my belief system to find the foundation I would rebuild from. I set aside long-held beliefs and started getting curious as to why I had believed them. I was searching for my identity, but ended up discovering that it is a part of God's creation! I discovered His design for me was as unique as the story of my life. I discovered that He wants a relationship with me, probably even more than I have wanted it with Him! I discovered a love that needs to be learned through encounters and experiences. A love that when shared, literally transforms lives.

I had believed that I had to give my heart to Jesus, but I discovered that He was already there! He was already building, already living, already breathing, already loving in and through me. My original belief system had told me this needed to be fought for, but this is not what I discovered. We are not called to fight in a battle that is already won, we are called to love. It's not complicated, but my belief system made it that way. I have believed for years that I'm nothing more than a sinner, but now I know that this is the last thing that God would ever want to call me.

At the moment we hear many speak of transformation. I've always found myself wondering what "transformation" actually was designed to look like through God's eyes. I hope we will begin to see it happen tangibly in our lives, where *transformation* isn't just a word, it's a testimony.

It was the most beautiful thing when I experienced a relationship with God, where nothing separated our hearts. It was there that I discovered deep unity and great love. It was there that I discovered safety and truth. It's there that faith, hope, and love exist and thrive!

Through Jesus, everything that prevented us from gaining access to Eden (God's heart), has now been removed and we have unrestricted and unhindered access.

The Garden of Eden is a place of mystical beauty and wonder, a place that is often looked upon as fiction. We are many years outside of the time when Adam and Eve walked on our planet, but I believe the encounter of love that God gave them every single day was real and powerful. I believe in a place where we no longer need to hide, a place where we can be seen and known for who God created us to be. Eden was a real place.

I was asked recently if rather than Eden, could God be leading us back to the metaphorical Promised Land, the place that the Bible calls "a land flowing with milk and honey" (Exod 3:8), the land that He promised to the Israelites when they left Egypt. This land was also mystical and full of wonder to the Israelites. Through Moses, God released His power and His plan for His people to have a land to call home. When they got to this land, Moses sent spies in and charged them to explore what the land was like and who occupied it. They returned so excited for the abundant produce of the land, but so fearful of those who occupied the land. It was only Joshua and Caleb that returned with similar stories of the produce, but unafraid of those who occupied the land. We need more Joshuas and Calebs.

As I thought through where God was leading us, I realised the difference between the Promised Land and Eden. The Promised Land offered abundance and a home, but Eden offers us a relationship with God. It offers a place where sin no longer hinders us from the discovery that God wants to be in a relationship with us. We don't need to travel to the Middle East to rediscover or claim this land. We only need to fall in love with God.

In July of 2019, I was invited to join a team of people to see what Lebanese Christians are doing in response to the Syrian crisis. Lebanon, to me, is a country of contradictions. It is both profoundly beautiful and profoundly chaotic. There is so much turmoil, but again, there is so much resilience. We were there with *Transform Aid*, an aid organisation operating out of Australia. The invitation to go came with a request to help them discern what God was doing through the local partners there on the ground.

Before we left, we were told this was one of the greatest humanitarian crises currently in the world. We were also told that it was a dangerous place to visit. Historically, the region has always seemed to be unstable, but with the ongoing Syrian Crisis unfolding next to it, we knew it would be an interesting visit. Before leaving, we had a security briefing where we were instructed to write a proof of life letter! I didn't even know what that was! It was writing a series of questions and answers that only Trish, my wife, would know. It was a bit scary. However, amid all that chaos, we knew God was up to something.

Approximately two million Syrian refugees have been displaced by the Syrian Crisis which started back in 2011. There still aren't many solutions. I had never been to the Middle East, so everything that I encountered there was new to me. I'd heard a lot about Lebanese culture, the food, their religions, their civil war, and the way that they do family. But none of my expectations prepared me for what I encountered in Lebanon!

To say that Lebanon is beautiful is an understatement, and doesn't do the country justice. It is a country of magnificent mountains that sits right on the Mediterranean Sea. Just to be a tourist in this country is something that I never dreamed of doing, but I was so glad to see the beauty and wonder of it. It has an incredible and painful history. It is a country that seems to be unafraid to show its scars.

All around Lebanon the buildings are derelict and bullet-ridden. It was leftovers from a brutal civil war that seemed to affect every person I talked to in some deeply traumatic way. It is a country that has a political system built upon religion, both Christian and Muslim. Although most people I spoke to were not optimistic about the way the country was being run, they had ways of coping with it. The people of Lebanon are enormously generous and hospitable. They love to eat and they love to feed you food that treats your tastebuds. I found people who had a deep joy for life, regardless of the journey they had experienced.

Generally, the refugees we met had similar stories. War had driven them from their homeland, and most had lost everything. They'd lost family members, their identity, their dignity, their hope, and their security. Many did not know where their partners were, or if they were alive. They did not know if their men were fighting for Syria, or even being forced to fight for ISIS. Every story was so similar. Lebanon didn't seem to want them, so the government made gaining refugee status torturously difficult. I found myself heartbroken for these people and in disbelief that people could do what I was repeatedly hearing to other people. These stories would be hard to exaggerate in their severity. But it was here that I saw the love of God do what no other force on the planet could do. Each day brought with it new encounters, but the one that changed my life happened on the second day we were there.

We were going into one of the slum areas of Beirut. It was an area that you could smell before you could see it. It wasn't quite a garbage dump, but it was close. We drove in through the big steel gate of a walled-off facility. This particular organisation was there to rebuild communities, not just build an infrastructure to house displaced people. They were there to restore dignity and honour to people. They were there to care and teach. They were there to love people. They showed us around the school they were running. Over two hundred children attended there. As the Syrians in Lebanon were officially 'displaced people', they were not allowed to have access to school, healthcare, social services, or work. All the kids that came to the school were from families who fell into this category.

The staff we met were so compassionate. We could feel the love they had for the people they were serving. Years of their lives and their careers had been invested into these people, and we could see the fruit of it. With every family we met, the staff knew their names, their children's names, their stories, and their needs. There was a love there that was not based on what an organisation could give to them. It was a love that was changing every life associated with this work, both Syrian and staff members alike. We even met two local television celebrities that had given up their time to teach at the school. We could sense the children felt safe, as we could see the joy that flowed from them.

We saw the medical centre the organisation had established, followed by the mental health facility. Then we observed the vocational centre in full swing. In each place we visited, we saw the work of this local organisation restoring the hope and dignity of a people that had every reason to have none.

This all preceded a greater encounter for me. Near the end of the tour, we were asked if we wanted to go for a walk around the neighbourhood. As we wandered, we could see flags flying over houses that signified the protection that local groups of people gave to homes and businesses. We were told of a sewerage system that occasionally worked and a water supply that was saltwater. The injuries most commonly seen at the medical centre were rat bites. It is hard to describe how real this was and how families were making their homes in this place. Four of us, three from the team and a person who worked for the local organisation, were meeting Syrian families. We stopped at one place to meet a woman and four of her children. She had a friend with her at the time, who had two children of her own. She invited us into her home, which consisted of two small rooms. The second room we didn't go into, but the first one contained only a three-inch deep mattress, an old table and timeworn TV. As guests, we were given the mattress to sit on. It was worn, thin, old, and a single size mattress which was the only thing in the room to sit on. The woman, her friend and their families sat on the floor.

We sat there and listened to this woman's story flow out of her. She had escaped from Syria with her four children. She didn't know where her husband was and had not seen him in weeks. She hoped he was most likely looking for work back in Syria. She was desperately hoping that he would get out of Syria and be reunited with her before he turned fighting age. The fighting age for men to be drafted into the Syrian Army was eighteen. At that point I looked at the four children, the oldest was six and the youngest was only a few months old. It does not take a mathematician to work out that this family started before the parents were twelve years old. It's hard to express what I felt when the reality of this moment impacted me.

Somewhere in the midst of this, I realised that the atmosphere of the room we were sitting in did not match what I thought it should be. This woman had every reason to be hopeless and fearful. We were told by the people that were showing us around that poverty is measured in the ability to communicate. This woman had no phone, which meant she had no access to family or money, yet the atmosphere that I was feeling was not hopeless. I was witnessing our guide and the way that she engaged with everyone in the room, knew all the children's names and all their needs. She listened to every word that flowed from the woman. All of a sudden, I realised that I was watching love: pure, simple, and powerful!

Our guide was fully present with the mother. Every question the mother asked about her situation was answered with truth and honour. I was watching love drive fear away right in front of me. Again, it is so hard to fully express what I was feeling and seeing. I do not often like to use the phrase "life-changing," as I think we can overuse it, but sitting on the mattress of this Syrian mother's home, I got to witness God's love in all of its life-changing power!

As we left the home, I turned to one of the other team members, who was the chairman of the board of the organisation that I was travelling with. He said to me, "Did you feel that there?" He told me that, in his role, he had been on many trips like this but he'd never felt anything like that. I was so overwhelmed that what I was feeling was also being felt by each person in the room. It was so tangible, and transforming lives right in front of us. This love was restoring honour and dignity.

The power of this love created a safe place for questions to be asked and answers to be given with respect. Some of the mother's questions didn't get the answers she wanted, and yet, there was still such honour in the room. This love brought safety to a family who was driven in fear from their homeland by war. In all this chaos, I found myself somehow walking in a moment of love that I'd not felt before. It sounded a lot like the Garden of Eden to me.

Here nothing separated them from the love of God. Safety and grace had become powerful expressions of His Kingdom and His presence. In this brief moment of the mother's life, I knew I was witnessing perfect love casting out fear. I was watching God raise up people to love unconditionally. These Syrian refugees had nothing to offer; and yet, they were met with a love that was changing lives. I only spent a few days in Lebanon, but in that time I understood that love is not just the right thing to be doing, but the *most important* thing we need to be doing. God IS love, and as He is, so are we.

Right there in the middle of a poverty-stricken area of Beirut, I discovered Eden and the Father's heart. At that moment I realised Eden is the Father's heart. The place where love drives fear away and people discover their identity and design. It's the place where you can discover the richness and power of the love the Father has for you. I came back from Lebanon with such a fire in my heart for how powerful love is.

This was more than just an understanding or a knowledge of love, this was an experience, a revelation and transformation all wrapped up in one. For me, it was an opening to discover the Father's heart in ways that I had only ever wondered about. Here is where transformation became more than a word, it became my story and my testimony.

To learn to see someone as God sees them
is an act of love that is as normal as breathing

EDEN: OUR BEGINNING

In writing a book about Eden, I'm sure that some will wonder why we need to go that far back to understand what God is doing now. For me, the answer is simple. If we want to know where we're heading, we need to understand where we have come from. In understanding where we have come from, we begin to understand the design. If we believe we have a design, then we must believe that we have a Designer. If the Designer has a purpose, then His plan will be discovered in His design. If He has a plan for my life, then I need to understand the design of my life first.

I've always believed that God's transformation of me was His plan. What I struggled with was seeing His design for me. The Bible is full of help with this. It starts with understanding whose image we have been created in. We were created in the image of God, who is the Father, Son, and Holy Spirit. I believe that this transformation or design leads us to become more like the man Jesus as if we are Jesus (Luke 6:40). It leads us to knowing that He lives within us, and we live with-

1

in Him (John 15:4). I'm believing that He has lifted us to the level of His family (Luke 18:21), and we are bound to His family by His blood (Rom 5:9) which was shed for us on His cross. Our thinking needs to start from the place of knowing that we have the mind of Christ (1 Cor 2:16) and that He has invited us to do even greater things than He has done (John 14:12), simply by loving others and ourselves as He has loved us (John 13:34). These are the incredible words of Jesus from scripture, which tell us that we are on this planet to do even more than He has done and to become all that He has created us to be.

But it all starts back at the start of the world, and as the Bible tells it, we start in the Garden of Eden. In Genesis 1 and 2, we read of the power of our Creator and we see the character of our Creator. The creation that He designed became the creation that would reproduce and thrive. We saw His goodness and we saw His image; the image of whom we were created in. From Chapter 2 of Genesis, we saw that relationships, with both Him and others, were always a part of His design.

His design can be seen so clearly in Eden. It's there that He created perfection. Everything He created He declared to be good. Right from the birth of our existence, His goodness and character were being sown into everything that surrounds us today. It was there that He created freedom, purpose, and identity. Freedom looked like the ability to do whatever we wanted. Purpose looked like being fruitful and multiplying. Identity looked like Adam and Eve understanding who they were. And most importantly, it was there that He invited them to choose a relationship with Him. He chose to walk with Adam and Eve as He would walk with us. He spoke to them, led them, directed them, and gave them the understanding of what clinging to His words looked like. So rich was this place of relationship, that it could be seen that nothing separated them from God's love. God was so intentional

2

in this. He gave them authority over all of His creation. God trusted them with it, as He is trusting us with it today.

The significance of this should not be lost or understated. Through Jesus' death, God gave us an amazing insight into how far-reaching this sacrifice would go. God was removing the curtain that separated us from Himself and allowed us again to see His heart and hear His voice for ourselves. This is our Eden; this is the place where He reveals Himself to us. It is safe, it is transforming, and it is loving.

These are often the last words that people use to describe churches these days. Churches have become known more for judgment, or lack of judgment, rather than for love. I think this is a natural flow-on effect from generations of being told what God has said rather than hearing what God has said, and it needs to change. Jesus didn't need an army to change the world, He needed a bunch of friends that would walk with Him. He didn't need huge strategies or five-year plans, He just modeled a safe life, transforming and loving. As we can read in history, and not just in the Bible, people came from all over the known world to encounter One who just chose to be present with people.

So much of the world's wisdom comes against the Church in the terms that we believe in fiction or fairy tales. Like I said earlier, I've heard people, even Christians, speak of the physical Eden as a place of mythology or ideology. If we choose to believe this, we can easily believe that the spiritual place of Eden is also purely a myth or an ideal. If you keep following this thought process you can then conclude that most of the messages that we teach and preach are speaking about a myth and not a reality. We cannot preach of the abundance and fullness of God, without believing that these are real expressions of who God is and what He is inviting us into. I believe that Eden was not only real, it was the design that He gave to us to live in every area of our lives.

3

Since I wasn't alive back then, when I read Genesis 1 & 2, it is my imagination that paints the pictures that I believe it to be. I may get to Heaven and discover that my imagination wasn't even close to reality. But as I imagine what I read, I see His character clearly in His design. I also know that He is the same yesterday, today and forever (Heb 13:8). Therefore, what I encounter of Him today would have been encountered by Adam and Eve in Eden.

I understand that it got messy for them once they started making choices they'd wished they hadn't made. I'll talk more about that in the chapters to come. But even in poor choices, God's design doesn't change and His M.O. is constant; He is all about relationships.

It's this original design that has captured my heart and attention. I think I've lived most of life from a false belief that Adam and Eve's sin brought about a fracture in our world that would not be restored until Jesus came back again. So bad was that sin that all of humanity was destined to live in some form of dysfunctional relationship with God forever. We know that Jesus' death and resurrection was to bring about the solution. However, I still unwittingly believed that it wouldn't be until I reached Heaven that I could see the fullness of who He is. I guess religion had convinced me that this was the one and only plan. Only curiosity led me to discover that this wasn't the plan all along! It just didn't make sense to me. The question I kept asking myself was, "Why show us the original design if we weren't designed to live by it?"

Then the next question that I had to come to grips with was, "How powerful was Jesus' sacrifice and resurrection?" We speak of it as if nothing more powerful has happened to the world, but often I would live from the belief that its power would only be seen in Heaven.

Something just didn't add up for me. There had to be more, and it had to be real. I felt that I was being led like a donkey with a carrot dangling, only to realise that I don't even like carrots that much! If religion was all about just dangling this carrot of Heaven in front of me to keep me moving towards this one divine moment... then I was out. Again, there had to be more.

Before I pastored at a church, I worked in structural and civil engineering. So, I know a thing or two about designing structures. I know that when we designed a bridge or a building, we didn't have multiple designs. We had one brief, and in that brief, we were given the picture of the structure that the architect wanted to build. The last thing that we would have done, would have been to give the builder two different designs and invited them to build whichever one they prefered. They were given one and if they wanted the structure to stand up, they needed to follow the design. God, in Eden, gave us one design and that design has never changed; He designed us to be in a relationship with Him. That relationship would be marked by the love that we shared for all eternity.

This love is the foundation stone for all that He designed and created. This same love brought Jesus to earth from Heaven. It is the same love that He invited us to build strong and resilient lives upon. Lives that would overcome failure and mistakes with love. Lives that would learn and grow in the love that we were designed to live by. This, to me, is the simple plan that God handed Adam and Eve all those years ago.

Our choice to let go of this relationship indeed messed with the plan, but it could not change the design. In engineering, if someone messes with the design, they mess with the outcome of the plan. Lives are put at risk. Architectural hopes get dashed. Also, the useability of the structure is severely compromised. If it's too far from the design, the structure may have to be completely torn down and restarted. If it was restarted, the engineers would be insisting that the original design is being adhered to. When Adam and Eve started messing with the design, the outworking of the plan shifted. But what didn't shift was God's desire to 'do relationship' with us. In Jesus' life, we were being given a clear example of a life lived following the original design.

Can you use your imagination to see Jesus walking into the synagogue just like God walked into Eden looking for Adam and Eve? He wasn't there to condemn them, but to save them. He wasn't there to pour down God's wrath, but to pour out His love. Even with such great mockery and accusation that came against Him, He still loved, healed, and restored all who came to Him. Jesus' life was like watching creation happen all over again, His love was making all things new.

So what messes with the design today? What keeps us from believing that a relationship like Jesus enjoyed with the Father is also God's plan for us? What I've seen taught for years in the church is the power that sin has brought into our world. God called that power 'death' and from the days of Eden, this word has been feared. It is what we fear that can so easily control us, and and in doing so we are forever giving power to it.

The church has been particularly good at emphasising the fear of death. For generations, people were taught it and controlled by it. The fear of death was used to scare people away from or out of hell. On my recent trip to England, I saw so much medieval art framed around this kind of fear. One particular piece stood out to me and it was titled, *The Cauldron of Souls*. It was a stone carving of a cauldron filled with people going to hell with Satan stoking the fires beneath

6

it. Every part of this art piece was horrific to the viewer. I'm sure that was the purpose of it. As a preacher, we love to use props to illustrate our point. It wasn't hard to see the point of this piece of art. Death has power, and it is a power that we would rarely encounter positively.

You have probably heard of "fire and brimstone" preaching. This phrase was born from a place where fear would drive people to the gates of Heaven. The preacher would often use graphic depictions and metaphors of how horrific hell was in the attempt to convince a person that choosing God would deliver them from it. As far as evangelistic strategy goes, this isn't one that I believe helps demonstrate the love of God. I'm not saying that hell doesn't exist, or isn't as horrific as the way Jesus described it in the Bible. But what I am saying is that it's far better to love someone into the Kingdom, rather than scare a person out of hell. I've always found that fear is temporal, where love is an eternal power that will never die.

It's not hard to see that fear is not a character trait of God. It wasn't present in Eden until Adam and Eve effectively invited it in and decided to let go of what God was offering them. Fear was also not a character trait of Jesus. It wasn't fear that drew crowds of people to Him. It wasn't fear that cast out demons or healed the sick; it was love. People felt safe to be around Him. Parents felt safe to let their kids sit on His lap. Lepers didn't fear the risk of being called "unclean," rather they came to Him for healing that was for more than a skin disease. A woman feels safe to cry tears onto His feet, all the while Pharisees are condemning her. This is the power of love at work; it changes lives eternally.

With fear so often being a theme of the church's preaching, is there any wonder as to why people are leaving the church in droves? God's

7

original design was truly being messed with. We have developed major teachings on sin and its effects, but we have been light on the, infinitely more powerful, love of God. Why have we been taught of how sin has separated us from God when the Bible tells us very clearly that nothing separates us from God? What might have been true before Jesus' sacrifice is no longer true after it. Through His grace and His love, He is looking for our belief and love, not for our sins. Everything we do, when done from love, will lead us further and further into transformation and relationship with God.

I don't say this to diminish sin, I say it because I believe God is leading His Church into a supernatural shift to understand the power of His grace and His love. This is God's original design, and He's making it understandable for us. His plan is seen so powerfully when Jesus was asked what the greatest commandment is in the Bible. He said, "'You must love the Lord your God with all your heart, all your soul, and all your mind.' This is the first and greatest commandment. A second is equally important: 'Love your neighbour as yourself.' The entire law and all the demands of the prophets are based on these two commandments" (Matt 22:37-40). Can you see here that Jesus has just wrapped up everything God said from Adam through the rest of the Old Testament in two phrases? It is all about love. It always has been and always will be.

EDEN: GETTING THERE

The journey into discovering these powerful truths started many years ago for me, pastoring a small church in the Inner West of Sydney. One of the key areas that I found myself ministering in was healing and deliverance prayer. It was a ministry that God had started with my earthly father, and I followed in his footsteps. It is a very beautiful thing to be a second-generation pastor. Watching my dad do life, family, and ministry was a learning gift. This kind of ministry was new to much of the Church. However, he felt commissioned by God to pioneer a work that would often have him ridiculed and accused of all kinds of religious wrongdoings. He counted a cost so that I could discover the Kingdom through love and power, and not through religion. It's a blessing that I will carry all the days of my life.

As I was growing in this understanding, I began noticing this past generation in church culture and congregations change. They became more transient than generational. No longer did people come to church every Sunday. They came when it suited the busy lifestyle which became a cultural necessity. I watched as church attendances all over my city shrank. I started looking for every concept of church growth that I could find. The temptation, for me, was to start following the worldly wisdom of church management rather than listening for God's voice. I found formulas and books of church growth, rather than pressing into God's heart and discovering His plan for His Bride. I found great programs that should have empowered community and purpose in the people I was serving. All of these programs had good aspects, but deep down I knew that there had to be more.

Through the healing and deliverance ministry, God was showing me obvious things about how He worked, but I was slow on the uptake. It took years before the penny dropped. I discovered that empowering people to live from their design was never about a program, it was always about relationships with God, ourselves, and each other.

Person after person was coming to me seeking freedom and to live a full life. I started to become aware that helping a person into freedom was merely the doorway to a full life. I was participating in one part of a divine process. People not only needed to be set free, they needed to hear God's voice for themselves. Then they were able to discover the power of actively living in relationships.

You see, we were created to be in a relationship with God. This was and is our design. We were created to speak with Him and listen to Him. We were created to see Him and interact with Him. Adam and Eve walked and talked with God, and we also have that as a foundation in our design.

However, the problem I have witnessed is that for generations people were taught that only a few could hear and see God. That is when I realised that people were coming to me to hear God speak and not listen for themselves. People would rely on me for words from God, which led to them relying on me for key decisions they were making for their lives.

So, my whole life shifted and I began helping people to hear as I hear and see as I see. I discovered that people were so eager to hear God's voice and be in a relationship with Him. They wanted to know love, to be loved, and to love others. All I was doing was helping them to see that this was our design from the beginning. It was always God's character and language.

The next discovery was that this God-designed relationship had very little to do with religion. Which led me to deconstruct my belief system to find the place where it was only Jesus and me. I found that as a church leader I was peddling theologies rather than building relationships. I was mimicking what I had seen go before me, rather than discovering what God had for me. I found that I had chosen to follow a theology or a program rather than trusting my ability to hear God for myself.

I just hadn't stopped for long enough to realise that my best efforts still came up short. I had tried to be holier, purer, hungrier, and more devoted. Each effort left me worn out or even burnt out. I've chased promises in the Bible, declared them and attempted to create them in my world. I've demanded things from God, without asking Him what He was doing. Each of these things left me wondering if the "abundant life" of John 10:10 was merely fiction. I have cast away demons. I've prophesied for the hundredfold blessing to be poured out. I've even gone back to the Old Testament and made Jabez' prayer my own. But still, this *abundant life* seemed to be just out of my reach. I wondered whether God was just messing with me by dangling a carrot in front of me that I was never going to reach.

I don't doubt that each of these efforts did some good for me. But what I was missing was the relationship. I wanted what Adam and Eve had in Eden with God. However, my best efforts had brought me to the conclusion that Eden was not tangible, and therefore not meant for me. How wrong I was. I have discovered so much since I accepted the invitation to enter Eden to rest in Him, to live in Him, to walk with Him, and to be in love with Him. I found love and grace. So much has changed.

I no longer sweat the small stuff of theology. I have become convinced that even our best theologies can't tie all the loose ends of God together. I've stopped judging people for what I saw as their lack of faith or making choices that I would have said led them away from God. From this position of love and grace, I found that a person's choices did not need to change the way that I love them. I found that I can even disagree with their choices and remain in a strong relationship.

I discovered my identity. I encountered God's love in ever-growing ways. My life began transforming, and the Garden of Eden became a reality. The more I lived from this place, the more I learned its language, which was truly unique.

Let me illustrate this through my experience. While I was in Lebanon, I quickly discovered that English was not widely spoken. Arabic and French were the common languages, with Arabic being the most common. Many times, I needed to rely on interpreters to understand the conversations that I was hearing. I'd never been in a country where I felt so helpless with communication. In Europe, they at least use the same alphabet and I can awkwardly pronounce a word that may be remotely close to what I want. But in Lebanon, the Arabic language was not something that I could get close to. I'd learned some key words; like *hello*, *thank you*, and *let's go*, which were easy enough to be able to parrot. But I was having trouble with any words more than that.

If I wanted to communicate properly, I needed to learn the language, and that wouldn't happen in the two weeks I was there. On top of this, there were different dialects for different areas. There were times we were with Syrian refugees living in Lebanon and they too, although speaking Arabic, had their dialect as well. I realised that if I was going to be able to communicate with the people then I had to find a way to submerge myself in the culture of the people. The Arabic language is beautiful to listen to, and I found that there was a rhythm to the way they spoke. It made me want to learn to be able to speak like them.

Among all of this, I heard God speak about His Kingdom and the language of Eden. You see, like with the few words of Arabic that I had learned, I could parrot the phrases of Jesus or of the Church. However, if I wanted to understand and speak the language, I needed to submerge myself in the culture of the Kingdom.

In John 10:16, Jesus says that His sheep will know His voice. I knew that this was something that I desperately wanted. But to know His voice, was to learn the language that He spoke. It was to learn that voice so that I could know His mood by the tone of the voice that I heard. This was the voice that Adam and Eve listened to in Eden. They walked with the owner of the voice, learned His language, and grew to speak it fluently.

I can only wonder how many more relationships I could have developed in Lebanon if I had known the language. I wonder how many more stories I could have listened to, or even, how many meals I could have ordered for myself! Not knowing the language prevented me from understanding and communicating more.

I came out of Lebanon wondering about my relationship with God. I found that I had used His words like they were a recipe. I was believing that if I used them in the right way, God would hear and interact with my prayer. I do know that He heard them, but I now know that I wasn't listening for Him to speak to me. I needed to learn His language. I didn't just want to meet Him as Adam did in Eden in the cool of the evening. I wanted to speak to Him, listen to Him, see Him, love Him, and grow with Him.

Jesus invited us all into this kind of relationship. It's something that He modeled for the disciples. In Luke 5:16 it says, "Jesus often withdrew to the wilderness for prayer." Now in our culture, we call the *wilderness* a bad place, a place of suffering or loneliness. However, in Jesus' time, this was anything but that. After being in the Middle East, it's quite obvious to see that the wilderness is often not far from where you are. I'm sure back in the first century it was even more accessible than what I saw. So Jesus would duck out to spend time with His Heavenly Dad.

We call this prayer, but I wonder whether our traditional understanding of prayer is what Jesus was thinking. With Jesus, it was a dialogue, not some kind of Lord's Prayer monologue. Jesus told His disciples that He only spoke what He heard the Father saying (John 12:49) and He only did what He saw the Father doing (John 5:19). These times of prayer in the wilderness were a whole lot more than finding a quiet

14

place to monologue with God. To understand the language that Jesus spoke with the Father was to spend time in the culture of the Kingdom of God. Could this be why Jesus was so big on teaching people about the Kingdom of God?

It's important to note that there were two languages being spoken in Eden. One in particular was destructive and had the sound of death. I call this a talking snake. A very important lesson for every person to learn is that reasoning with the Devil, as Eve did, only ever leads you away from God's voice and heart, never toward it.

The Devil's goal is always to have you doubting the very things that God is speaking to you. It was doubt of God's voice that he sowed into Eve. Once doubt was seeded, as the Apostle James says, she became "unsettled as a wave of the sea that is blown and tossed by the wind" (James 1:6). Eve had become that unsettled wave which crashed into Adam. Doubt is contagious and has a habit of leading us down pathways we would not normally choose. The pathway that Adam and Eve chose would lead them away from God's voice and out of Eden.

New feelings and emotions would have been flooding through their systems after eating the fruit from the Tree of Knowledge of Good and Evil. They were feeling fear for the first time and shame had them hiding for the first time. Even now, we can be so easily confused when our fears that control us and the shame of our mistakes combine. In that confusion we can very easily slip into a thinking that has us second guessing whether God's love is real. We start thinking more of judgment than we do forgiveness. We learn a language that sounds a lot like condemnation than grace. It doesn't take a person much time to get confused when listening to the language that comes out of many of our churches. We're told that we are loved and forgiven, but then we're told in the same breath what we must do to be and stay loved and forgiven.

The Devil's language and his kingdom feeds off doubt, fear, death, and shame. It's a language that whole cultures can quickly adopt and speak. It was a language that Adam and Eve discovered after they had chosen to speak when they were standing in front of God. When God asked them what had happened, a conversation of blame started flowing from Adam to Eve and then to a snake. They were standing in front of Him ashamed of the creation that He had made. They sought to hide it from God and each other. This is a language and behaviour that we are still doing today.

Why God allowed the Devil to be in Eden in the first place is one of those conversations that I'm keen to have with Him. But what I know is that even in Eden, God gave us the ability to listen to and discern other voices. He gave us the ability to choose to cling to His words of life as much as He gave us the opportunity to let them go. Choice, for me, is one of the fundamentals of a loving relationship. If there is no freedom of choice, then there is no place for love. What we are left with is simply control and one party must do what the other says. Where there is love there is choice. The choice empowers the voice within each person, which becomes a mechanism for love to grow and be seen in.

I have also discovered the voices that we hear the most we will recognize the most. Years ago, in one of my sermons, I had a person stand at the front of the church with their back to the people. I then had arranged for a few people to speak to him. Some he had known for a long time and others for less. He was instantly able to recognize those he knew well. He found it more difficult to recognize those he was less familiar with. It was a great way to demonstrate the power of a relationship.

I think it speaks directly into our relationship with God. I asked myself, "Would I recognise him if He came up behind me and spoke to me?" In the sermon activity, I could see the instantaneous recognition and resulting joy on the person's face. He only needed to hear the voice to know the relationship that he shared with that person. If the relationship was love, then love was seen in the reaction.

Through my discovery of God's voice and our resulting relationship came the desire to lead others to this same understanding of the relationship. The beautiful thing is that each person I meet has a different story, and a different lens they see life through. This gives us the brilliant opportunity to love each person uniquely without judgment through grace, as Jesus did. He didn't engage with Nicodemus the same way He engaged with Mary Magdalene. They had completely different stories and perspectives. But to each, He was present and spoke to their hearts. We get to love each person uniquely with grace, as God does.

We love most powerfully when we love the person in front of us uniquely. If you love someone, you do not generalise their story or their experiences. A person you love goes beyond race, religion, age, and choices they have made in life. If I generalise a person's story then I have stopped loving them, and I have begun weighing them up by what I know of their culture or their choices and not their God-given design.

Generalising is an easy thing to do, even in churches. There are things we need doing and we look for people to do them. But if we let things become the priority, we will tend to value people by what they can do.

This culture needs to change in our churches if we want to see relationships flourishing.

Relationships can be easily tested by the fruit they produce in critical moments. Finding "love, joy, peace, patience, kindness, goodness, faithfulness, gentleness, and self-control" (Gal 5:22-23) in a relationship, even during difficult times, is what Jesus Himself modeled and invited us into. Paul calls these the fruits of the Holy Spirit, giving us a brilliant way to test the relationships we have. If they're producing these things, then we are watching the Holy Spirit at work.

Let's go a little further with this. In Matthew 16:19, Jesus gives the Apostle Peter the Keys of the Kingdom. In this one verse there is an extraordinary understanding of the authority and language of the Kingdom of God. It would have been awesome if the Gospel writers had given us more information about what Jesus was referring to with these keys! The concept of Jesus giving Peter keys must point to having authority to either lock away or release. The keys were given to Peter after Jesus asked the disciples to speak out who they believed Him to be. Peter simply replied, "You are the Messiah, the Son of the Living God" (Matt 16:16). A powerful moment of faith was met with an empowering upgrade in understanding the love and trust that Jesus was giving to Peter.

Peter had immersed himself in the culture of the Kingdom and had discovered the King. Jesus invited him into this place of relationship so that he could be immersed in it, and Peter had accepted the invitation. Peter was speaking Jesus' language! As Jesus had loved him, so had he loved Jesus. It needed to start somewhere. Jesus coming to Peter and asking him to follow Him was akin to God coming into the Garden and looking for Adam and Eve.

As the love built between them, so did the trust. Jesus was witnessing faith grow inside of Peter through the love that He had invested in him. Sure, there were questions that Peter had and mistakes he made along the way; however, all of these seemed to draw Jesus closer to Peter. Peter is one of the biblical characters that I connect with strongly. I'm sure that's because he's the one who messes everything up and still finds himself so close to Jesus. Through Peter we get to see grace and love in tangible ways.

Then when Jesus gives Peter the keys to the Kingdom, I believe he's effectively saying, "well done, my good and faithful servant. You have been faithful in handling this small amount, so now I will give you many more responsibilities. Let's celebrate together!" Jesus wanted to celebrate with him! He wanted to celebrate their relationship and give him access to everything in the Kingdom. Keys represent access to locked away places and I can sense Jesus' excitement for all that Peter would discover as he used them!

So what are those keys and why was it so important to Jesus for Peter to receive them? I believe that the keys are bound to the language of the Kingdom and are also found in Eden. Here's what two of those keys look like in my life (and maybe yours): To love and to listen. Two things Jesus has done and is doing for me. Now, they are two things I desire to do every day of my life, to love and listen to God and others. In loving a person, I am creating a safe and judgment free place for them to exist in. In listening to them, I am investing my life in theirs; I am effectively inviting them into my heart and life. It's in this place that I discover the unique person I am in a relationship with. In this place, love can unlock a whole range of things that had prevented someone from growing and transforming.

I think it's a part of our human design to be seen and heard. However, sometimes life drives us into places of hiding and fear, like Adam and Eve. We then protect ourselves and our hearts from others judging us, or worse, condemning us for the things that have happened to us or the choices we have made. When someone feels safe enough to share their heart with you, it is clear that you have been given a rare gift to see them as they see themselves. Adam and Eve hid from being seen by God for fear of shame. This is why I love Jesus so much; even when I was hiding, He came looking for me. When we do the same for others who are hiding away their lives for fear of shame, we are inviting them to come out of hiding and into healing.

We live in a time where we seem to generalise people, places, communities, churches, governments, and pretty much everything. In doing so, we form opinions based on people group assumptions and are not open to loving unique people. For example, if someone attends a particular church that is known for a ministry, there can be a tendency to generalise the members and believe they must align with everything that the church appears to stand for. In other words, we're not using the Keys of the Kingdom, but the keys of culture and assumption.

It is an act of grace to love a person before you hear their story and it is an act of relationship to not let their story change the way you love them. If I make assumptions of a person before I listen to them, then I will form an opinion before I have had the chance to love them.
Any time that we assume something about someone, we are effectively trying to read their mind. This is never a helpful strategy for loving people. If we are loving them, we are giving them the place to be authentically known. However, by assuming and then creating an opinion of the person, we are demanding they behave the way we expect them to. In my opinion, this is manipulation. I want to invest

in people and see them live out of the fullness God has for them. We cannot love and manipulate someone at the same time.

Each time we love, the Kingdom of God advances and is released. Every. Single. Time. Every time we love, God is seen and a supernatural manifestation occurs. If you want to see God, then look for Him in the love that we share. He is there. He is present, tangible, and real. God can be seen.

There are so many of Jesus' encounters with people that speak to this truth. When He dines with tax collectors, He becomes the talk of the town. But it's what happens at the table with these tax collectors that's the real story. Love and transformation happen at these tables. Lives are changed eternally with these encounters. When Jesus reached out and touched lepers, all kinds of things were healed. His love heals and, before you know it, people everywhere are talking about Jesus. He stops and asks blind Bartimaeus, "What *can I do for you?*" His love stopped a whole crowd of people and suddenly people are seeing who Jesus is.

What is Jesus doing? He's giving us a working example of what love looks like and what love does. Love is designed to restore, but it's where that restoration is pointing us that I'm most interested in. Jesus said, "*I only do what I see my Father doing.*" What is God doing? He's loving His people and He's using His Son to love. Now He has invited us to do the very same things and greater things, as God continues to reveal what He's doing in Heaven. By showing us what love can do, He's leading us back to Eden.

Each act of love was a recreating of what existed at the start of creation. Jesus, in coming to earth, was an act of love that would restore

21

us into a tangible relationship with God. His life then became our working example that would challenge religion, culture, social status, and families. Jesus' fame grew from the miracles He was working, but the Kingdom grew from the love that He was walking in, a love that would change everything.

In 1 John 4:18 it says, "Such love has no fear because perfect love expels all fear." When John wrote this verse and sent it to the churches, he was testifying and not just prophesying. Here's a man who walked with Jesus and watched love drive fear away. He felt the atmosphere change when Jesus entered the conversation. Today we use this verse as prophecy and believe that love will do this in the present and the future. Here is one who watched and could testify to all who he had seen. People felt safe to be with and seen by Jesus. People were unafraid to come to Him and share what was on their hearts. Condemnation didn't flow from Him, as there was no condemnation in Him. Beautiful moments of peace were birthed in the lives and hearts of those who met Him.

Earlier in this chapter, I borrowed a phrase of Jesus and effectively gave it to Peter, of "well done good and faithful servant." We commonly call the story *The Parable of the Talents*. You can find it in Matthew 25:14-30. In it, Jesus tells a story about three people who each receive a gift. Most times we hear this story told, we interpret the gifts as monetary. I want to add a little creative license here, and instead of interpreting the story as monetary gifts, what if we saw them as gifts of love? We would then read that Jesus gave to three people, three different encounters of His love. He gave five encounters to one person, two to another, and then one to the last. The first one took their five encounters of love and loved people as he had been loved. He found by doing this, the love surrounding him multiplied and he had twice as

22

many relationships than he did before! The second did the same with the two encounters. He found that by loving people as he had been loved that his relationships doubled as well! This is extraordinary, but a realistic way of understanding how God has designed our lives to be in relationship with Him and others. The last, however, took his one encounter of love and did nothing with it. He even went to the extent of hiding that love away, so that no one saw it. His life was unchanged by the love that had been so freely given to him.

The outcome of the story was that the Master was so thrilled with the increase of love, that He gave the first two incredible places of authority. They'd loved as He'd loved, and the Master had seen that they could be trusted with His love and their world got bigger. The last, however, had the encounter removed from him. He hadn't received it, nor valued it in the first place, and he was living from a place as if it hadn't happened. His world got smaller. Nobody could see the encounter of love; and in hiding it, he couldn't see it either. From this, he made up a generalised story to convince himself of what the Master was really like. Once he did this, there was nothing to do with that encounter of love, other than bury it away.

I wonder though whether most of us who go to church would know what it is to encounter Jesus' love. For if we don't know what it is, then we won't know what to do with it. Maybe the guy who only received one portion had not ever encountered His love before. Maybe he didn't want to lose it or give any of it away for fear that it would run out. Then it hit me that this is the way that I had lived most of my life as a believer. I hadn't known what His love felt like. I'd been told through many sermons that Jesus loved me, but I had not encountered it. So I'd been given a gift without understanding the giver of the gift or the gift itself. And here's a thing I have discovered: you can't teach someone that they are loved, you have to show someone that they are loved.

The Apostle Paul taught us that you reap what you sow (Gal 6:7). I have discovered a very simple yet powerful truth in this verse: if you plant apple seeds, do not expect to harvest oranges. If you plant love, you will harvest love. If you plant condemnation, you will harvest condemnation. If you plant peace, then peace is what you will feast upon. These are simple design principles from Genesis 1 in the natural. Now we get to see the same principle happen in our relationships.

I have found that often people who have walked away from faith, or the church, have done so because they have been told it was love that the church was sowing, but for them the harvest was a feeling of being judged and condemned. In churches, we have often been taught for generations a version of love that lacks true understanding. This has led many to believe more in religion and the Law than in the love of Jesus. I often wondered if the church has become experts at hiding a love that was never designed to be hidden. We have become the guy who only got one talent in the parable. We've lost track of who the Father is and thus we have made up a generalised image that works for our theologies or circumstances.

For example, the children of Israel couldn't wait for 40 days when Moses was on Mount Sinai getting the 10 commandments, so they invented an image for God and worshipped that image. It turns out they thought He looked like a calf.

How often do we get frustrated with God's timing and invent new theologies to support our choices and our timeframe? In doing so, we show the world a very confused concept of who God is, which leads us to explain our God rather than encounter Him. Jesus Himself said that the world will know we are His disciples by the love that we have for each other (John 13:35), not by the ability we possess to explain God. We weren't made to hide our love, or to hide away from love. We were made to love and to be loved. Our world needs us to love as Jesus loves.

A while ago I was sitting with a man in my office, who wasn't a believer in Jesus, but was desperate to be free from the torment that was the story of his life. Through a series of very poor choices and a very difficult family of origin, his desperation drove him to the front door of a church. As I sat with him and listened to him, his whole story poured out. I could see the loneliness and the loss he was sitting in. He desperately wanted to be loved. He needed an encounter of Jesus' love.

Often when I'm helping people, I will ask them to use their imagination to help them understand some of the deeper truths about themselves. One of the ways that I do this is to ask them to visualise their heart as if it were a house. Our imagination is such a powerful gift to us, and on that day, it became a powerful tool for Jesus to love through.

I asked him to imagine his heart as if it were a house and to tell me the very first thing that dropped into his mind. He described a run-down shack which was falling to pieces. It was dirty, bare, and the front door was hanging off its hinges. He seemed ashamed of what he was imagining. I asked him to describe the internal features of the house, to which he spoke of very little furniture and dust everywhere. As he worked his way through the house, I asked him to see if he could find a dining table. Through tears, and without words, he nodded. After a while he said that it was big and old, but again it was bare. I then asked him if he could invite Jesus to sit at the table. Through tears, he said, "He is already there." He was then so overcome by emotion, that it took some minutes to ask him the next question, "Where are you?"

By this time, tears were flowing and the carpet beneath him was getting wet. He told me that he wasn't even in the same room as Jesus, but he was standing at the door in tears. Jesus was inviting him to sit beside Him at the table. By this stage, I could tell that whatever was happening in his imagination was becoming more than he could bear. So, I asked him to open his eyes and tell me what was happening. He told me that he couldn't sit at the table. So, I asked him, "Why not?" He simply said, "Because I am not worthy to sit there."

He spoke to me of sitting at Jesus' feet and just crying and crying because so much he had done in his life had brought dishonour to his family and himself. Shame was crushing him and preventing him from believing in the love that was sitting right in front of him. He wasn't sitting at Jesus' feet as Mary did in the Bible, it was simply that he didn't feel he deserved a seat at the same table as Jesus.

I asked him to describe what Jesus was doing. He told me that Jesus was telling him, "You are worthy." It's hard to express the emotion that was flowing through this man to hear Jesus say these words to him. I found myself crying as many tears as him. Jesus' love has this beautiful way of multiplying and affecting everyone who is sitting in an atmosphere like this.

By the end of the time together, he had not only sat with Jesus, but his imagination was now showing a house under restoration. This man had an encounter with Jesus' love that changed his life. The last time I saw him was a week later. He had a million questions, but he held on to one truth; Jesus loved him. I don't know what happened to him past this point, but I do know he encountered Jesus' love. He was allowed to feel, see, and encounter God's character. My prayer is that he has had further encounters of that love and he's leading others to the same place of worthiness and love.

So, where to from here? I humbly suggest that Jesus' two-thousand-year-old model of loving others as He has loved us, needs to be understood, embraced, and lived. We must go back to Him if we are to go forward with Him.

EDEN'S FIRST DILEMMA

Eden wasn't perfect as we like to think that Heaven is perfect. What I mean by that is that Eden had a talking snake; you probably won't find those in Heaven. Or if you do, they won't be trying to get you to dethrone God. But that wasn't the only issue that was challenging Adam. Long before he was contending with a talking snake, he was contending with something that every one of us deals with in our lives: loneliness.

It is a fundamental part of our design to be in a relationship. So what does that mean? Jesus, when asked for the greatest commandment, cited two commandments and said that they are as equally as important as each other. Simply put, He said that you can't have one without the other: we are to love God and love others as we love ourselves (Matt 22:37-39). So relationship is then understood to happen between you and God, you and others, and also with yourself. The relationship is known by the manifestation of love.

The first dilemma that Adam encountered was not the talking snake, it was the absence of relationship with others. There is one thing in the creation story that is declared "not good," that Adam was alone (Gen 2:18). The very word *good* in the Hebrew language is such an interesting word. It is two letters long and they combine to form the phrase "covenant with man." So everything that God created and declared good was put there for the relationship that He would have with humanity. So for something to be "not good," it means that God is seeing that it is not helping His creation fulfill His design.

Let's go a little deeper with the words. In the same verse, God says that Adam needs a helper. Again in the Hebrew this word is profoundly deeper than just having a helper in life. The word here for *helper* means more about accomplishing a purpose than it does about accomplishing a task. Eve's addition into this conversation wasn't merely to help in doing things, it was to accomplish the very purpose that God had placed people on the planet for. So what was the purpose, I hear you ask? To love Him, others, and yourself. Genesis 2 goes on to say that God looked for that *helper* in all of the other animals and yet found none that could fulfill His creation and establish His purpose. For God, it was back to creating, and as the narrative tells us, Eve was created from Adam.

This passage, about Eve's creation, is often recited in wedding services today, particularly with the phrase that "two shall become one." But I think that God was showing us something much deeper than simply marriage here. It's so interesting that from the one became two and then, through their relationship, the two would become one. The oneness of Adam and Eve would become the very vessel for God's purposes to be fulfilled through. They could not do this alone, they needed each other.

Although this is a passage that gets rolled out in many Christian marriage services, I don't think that this was the intention of God. It is more about the necessity of a relationship than a requirement of marriage. Jesus would show us this in the relationships He surrounded Himself with. When He started His ministry one of the very first things He did was gather people who would become one with Him. He spoke about it in John 15 when He said, "Remain in me, and I will remain in you" (John 15:4). He repeated it in John 17 when He was praying to the Father, "...they will be united just as we are" (John 17:11). We know that Jesus never married, but what He did have is many relationships that were "one" with Him. These relationships would fulfill the purpose that Jesus was born for!

We need other people in our lives. I've often heard Christians tell me that they don't need anyone else in their lives and that they are happy just to be with God. It would seem that Adam might have something to say about this conclusion. Adam walked with God and yet still God saw that something was missing from his life. For His design to be working properly, he needed other like-minded people to do life with. The very first relationship was two choosing to love God, each other, and themselves. As you can see, right from the early days of humanity, we needed to work out how to do relationships in a way that worked with our design. The powerful effect that we get from healthy relationships is unity.

It didn't take long for us to see what a relationship looked like when it didn't operate in its design. Eve eats from the Tree of Knowledge of Good and Evil. She offers it to Adam who partakes. All of a sudden they're experiencing their relationships with God, each other, and themselves in a whole new way. Shame became a voice between them. God would soon enter the narrative looking for them. Once He found them, He found that they were speaking a different language marked by blame. Adam blamed Eve, she then blamed the snake, which resulted in Adam and Eve's relationship being compromised.

On top of that, in blaming the snake for having influence over them, Adam lost his God-given dominion over the animals. It also meant that the unity of all the relationships was fractured. They were hiding from God, blaming each other, and they had lost their identity. It's not hard to see the effect that blame or shame has on relationships. It brings disunity and loss of connection. It isolates and puts people into places of condemnation and judgment, which then brings us back to loneliness. This shows us that we are no longer operating from our design. We go back to a place of "not good," and the only helping being done is helping ourselves to survive fear instead of walking in mutual purpose.

When we find that we are judging more than loving in our relationships, we should stop for a moment and look to see what's gone wrong with our design. Jesus warned us against judging. He made it clear that any offence you see in others might be a reflection of your own behaviour, being the plank in your own eye preventing you from seeing clearly. In fact, if you read the Sermon on the Mount that Jesus gave, you will hear a whole message on living from the place of our original design. It's not just for our individual living, it's for us as we seek to love God, others, and ourselves well.

This is the plan the Church was given to once again be in a relationship with God. Somewhere along the way, the language started to shift and change. Somewhere along the way, we became comfortable with judging people. Somewhere along the way, we gave away our relationship with God and sought to hear Him through a few select, trained, and "qualified" people. Somewhere along the way, we became comfortable with a lesser form of living a full life.

We became convinced that instead of being created in God's image, we were created as sinners. We were told that we needed to invite Jesus into our lives when the Bible is full of Jesus inviting us into His. We were told that we needed to follow the rules of religion to get us to God, instead of following the voice of the One who speaks to us. Shame then became the tool that so many used for evangelism. There was a thought that if we told people how bad they were they would seek to do something about it. Instead, we should have been loving people into a place where they know how truly loved they are.

This raised the question, "Is it easier to judge people than to love people?" To which the answer was often that judging was easier than loving. However, this isn't the way we were designed. Any time you judge a person that you are in a relationship with, a little bit of life disappears from that relationship. To judge is to elevate yourself above others. It is to believe that you have all the wisdom needed for the relationship, which takes at least two. Eventually, if this is the normal way you do relationships, you will find yourself with few friends and in a place of loneliness.

I've watched this happen in my own life. When I was younger and had a much higher value on my ego, I wouldn't hesitate in declaring what was right or wrong. People kept leaving my life, and somewhere in my pride, I would declare that I was better off without them. Not every one that surrounds you are the "helpers" that Genesis 2 talks about. Some will be there for a season and some will be there for a lifetime. But when I turned around and asked myself the question, "Why am I so lonely?", there was only one person who could take responsibility for that—me. Now I have discovered that my role is simply to love people and to leave the judging and convicting of everyone to God. Again, it is far more valuable to love a person than to judge a person.

Preaching to people about how bad they are isolates and shames them. It tells them they are far away from God. This automatically removes unity, and the relationship between them and God shifts from a partnership to behavioural management. To do this to people takes us and them out of God's design. As this language was reinforced generationally, we grew up believing God was more about punishing us for poor behaviour than loving us for who He created us to be. This led us to believe that good behaviour got God's attention, rather than simply just believing in Him. This kind of belief system is more aligned with religion or even karma than it is with Jesus. It says that if I do good, then there should be some kind of reward that looks like goodness. If I do bad, then there will be some kind of consequence of badness. This was no thought of God's design for us.

I have watched this kind of "religion" take the place of relationships in my own life. As a leader, the choices and decisions I made would be more about the platform that I was building than loving the people that God placed in front of me. Jesus addressed this when He challenged the Pharisees, "For you are careful to tithe even the tiniest income from your herb gardens, but you ignore the more important aspects of the law—justice, mercy, and faith. You should tithe, yes, but do not neglect the more important things" (Matt 23:23). It was that phrase "the more important things" that got me. Jesus isn't doing away with all their religious practices, He simply is pointing them back to the Father's heart and character.

Nicodemus, Jairus, and Paul are the most notable Pharisees that heard this challenge. They made the tremendous step to change their belief system and align themselves to the Father's character and His Son. Nicodemus did it under the cover of darkness. He started from asking Jesus questions that led him to answers that he had not even thought about. Jairus came to it through the circumstances of life. When his daughter was deathly ill and no doctor could help him, he laid down all of his pride and asked Jesus to heal her. Paul, seemingly the most arrogant of them all, had an encounter with Jesus on the road to Damascus where he was invited to believe in the very one that he was trying to eradicate from the Middle East. All three educated and qualified men had discovered something in relationship with Jesus that they had not found in their own religion.

The "helper" from Genesis 2 is now seen in the way that these men would partner with Jesus. We don't hear any more from Jairus in scripture, but Nicodemus shows up two more times in John. The first is when the Pharisees are gathering to plan Jesus' death and Nicodemus speaks up for Jesus to be subsequently mocked for it. Then Nicodemus is found at the foot of Jesus' cross with Joseph of Arimathea where they receive the body of Christ. This one moment speaks so deeply of the oneness that Nicodemus had with Jesus. The Pharisees were demanding that anyone who followed Jesus was no longer welcome at the Temple. This was huge for the average Jew, but for a Pharisee, to follow Jesus was career and life changing. Nicodemus had found something that his religion could not offer him.

Then there was Paul, who went on to write most of the New Testament and then died for the very one that he had once tried to extinguish. These men had found that the fullness of life wasn't found in their careers or their religion, it was found right back in Genesis 2, when they encountered the oneness that came from partnering with Jesus. In fact, Paul would go further and list all of the accomplishments that his life had led him to. He weighed them all up and came to the conclusion that they were all nothing in comparison.

So here's the question that I was left with: Could loneliness be undone by simply living from our design? I'm willing to risk believing that if I love people as Jesus has loved me, then the lives of those I'm loving, including my own, will change. One of the great truths that I found is that people heal in safe relationships. Loving with grace and not judgment is the way that I've discovered to create safe relationships where people can be seen, heard, and known.

So, here's the challenge. I'm not sure churches are generally designed for this kind of thinking. In my experience I have found that churches are designed to gather people together that have similar values and mindsets. They do things that the majority of people are happy to do. They have budgets that need to be met and programs that the church thinks will draw people to them. In my own church, our service on a Sunday would normally run for 90 minutes. In that time, there would be singing, prophesying, and teaching. We have seen miracles, we have engaged with the presence of God, and seen lives transformed. We have been a part of so many encounters with the Holy Spirit that it would be difficult to count! Again, none of this is bad, but when it came time for a relationship, that all needed to happen in the 30-60 minutes after the service at our church's cafe. Again, this is not bad, but if all we do as a community is gather to do things to build the church community, we are missing the very essence of our design to love well.

Years ago I laid out the vision for my church. I was notoriously bad at creating vision. Each year would roll around with people looking for what we were going to do. What would we do for mission, for evangelism, for social justice, for discipleship, etc? As a solo pastor, this was overwhelming for me each year. I would sit with God and ask for the vision and get so frustrated with myself for not being able to coherently articulate what I thought would be inspiring for my church. Then all of a sudden I had an epiphany of sorts. The vision that would flow through me was the vision that included me.

So, I restarted the conversation with God over a coffee. As I sat there, I became very aware of the coffee in my hand. The one thing I love to do with people is to have a coffee with them. To sit face to face at a table and listen to their story. So at the church vision meeting, I spoke out that the vision for our church for that year was simply to have coffee with people, to love the one in front of you. I'd not given a vision statement like this before. Some thought it was just a joke knowing that I enjoy coffee as much as I do. But years later, this is the very vision that continues to unfold in front of me every day of my life. It calls me to sit with the ones that the Father has drawn to me, to listen to their story and value their voice, to love them as Jesus loves me. It is a relationship where two people become one, and both people are seen and heard. Adam and Eve found this with each other and God in the beginning.

GOD'S BIGGEST RISK

In my opinion, the biggest risk God took was on the sixth day, when He created us. Up until that time, everything He made would be self-sustaining and had been seen as "good." The introduction of humans created in His image would bring the creation story to a conclusion. Still, God "saw that it was very good."

He created us in His image. Here is the revelation of the design. He gave us something He did not give to anything else. We were created in His image. When we finally understand that this is what He planned for us, we will finally understand that we have value. We carry something that is eternal and is good.

There are a range of thoughts that go through my mind when I process this. Some of them would be close to what the church has traditionally declared to be heresy. My goal in writing this is not to promote division in the church, but rather to have a fresh look at an ancient design that theology has been seemingly trying to dismantle. The common way to do this is to replace the image of God with the sin of humankind. But the question that won't leave me is, "When did sin change the design?" I'm not denying that it affects the design, and it affects the design so significantly that God sent Jesus to do something about it.

It's here though that God's biggest risk can be seen. He gave us something that He knew we would struggle to understand...He gave us His image. The second question would be, "Why on earth would He have given us something we couldn't understand?" It was C.S. Lewis who would land on the answer when he said, "Of course God knew what would happen if they used their freedom the wrong way: apparently, He thought it worth the risk."

As a leader, it can be a risk to share leadership. It's a part of my design to look for people to share my leadership with. Sometimes that has worked powerfully well and other times, not so much. But I keep looking for people to partner and lead with. It has become one of the greatest joys of my life to release people to lead, to speak, and to teach. It is worth the risk.

In my early days of leadership, I didn't expect people to bring their baggage with them. I was naïve and had the skewed belief that they would be just like me. It sounds hilarious even writing this, but subconsciously it was the way that I worked. If it didn't get done my way, I would rant and throw tantrums until they either did it my way or left. Neither of these was healthy, and both destroyed more relationships than I was building.

God knew the risks of sharing His image and His authority with us, and still, He knew it was worth the risk. By now, I'm certain that you can see the risk that God took when He created us. When we are given a high level of authority, there is a great possibility to use that authority for something other than what it was given for.

When we elect politicians and leaders, we are giving authority to lead us and make decisions for us. Usually, that works well if they are making decisions that we agree with. When they are not, we are eager to find someone else who will make decisions aligned with our opinions. When God gave us His authority, other than a moment when we restarted the world with Noah, He has not withdrawn that authority from us. I believe that He has done this because of the value He placed on us on the sixth day. We were created for a relationship and oneness with Him.

I think if we have the understanding that God doesn't need us, or it's of no consequence to God if we do or don't want to come into that kind of relationship, we have missed one of the most powerful moments of our lives. God didn't just create us so that we would need Him. He created us to be in unity and love with Him. His desire to encounter us is even greater than our desire to encounter Him. But He is not a needy being that is codependent on us. He has invited us into a relationship where all things move with a rhythm that flows from a relationship that is working together in unity. Again, in God's opinion, it was worth the risk.

Humanity was created to be in a relationship with someone who loves us. To know the safety and strength of a relationship like this is to know the power of what a relationship like this can endure, persevere, and overcome. Sadly, though, millions of people go through their lives hoping for a relationship like this. Longing for a day when someone will see them and love them for who they are, not judge them for what they have done. Many have grown up in homes where the safety and strength of a relationship are nowhere to be seen. So they seek ways to keep themselves safe, rather than learning how healthy relationships operate. Survival becomes their understanding of a relationship.

People in Bible times were no different. Time and time again the Bible speaks of people doing what they felt was right. They had taken their authority and decided they could function outside of a relationship with God. They made decisions that were based more around their comfort, rather than on the benefits of having God in their lives. By Genesis 6, people had used this authority so poorly that it says, "The Lord observed the extent of human wickedness on the earth, and He saw everything they thought or imagined was consistently and totally evil" (Gen 6:5). It would seem at that moment as if God was wondering if it was all worth the risk.

It's then that we get to see His heart. We see that He is not some far-distant God who doesn't care for His creation. In Genesis 6:6 it says, "So the Lord was sorry that he had ever made them and put them on the earth. It broke his heart." Not all of us may know what it's like to grow up in a safe and loving environment, but all of us know what it is to have our hearts broken. Remember, we are made in His image and the very things that we feel, He is feeling as well. His heart broke...

When our hearts break, we look for solutions that seem to gravitate toward feeling less pain. He decided that getting rid of the source of His pain would fix the pain. In verse 7, God decides to start again. To start again was to destroy all that He had created.

Then in verse 8, it says, "But Noah found favour with God." I love this verse and I love the phrase, "But Noah." All of Heaven stopped in this moment of a person finding "favour with God." For Noah to find favour with God was not any great plan, it was simply to love God as he was loved by God. Often in our own lives, people find favour with us when they are doing something or behaving in a way that we expect. If they do so, we receive them. If they do not, we find ways to reject them. Finding favour with God is not about what we do, it's about who we are and who we're loving.

Verse 9 gives us an understanding of the man's character: "Noah was a righteous man, the only blameless person living on the earth at the time, and he walked in close fellowship with God." It's such a beautiful way of describing a person, and it sounds like Noah could well be found walking in the cool of the evening with God in Eden as Adam and Eve did. I used to read this thinking that Noah had not done anything wrong in his life, but that's not the case. To be blameless is to be forgiven. To be forgiven is to be invited deeper into a relationship. To walk with God was to know His voice and be at one with Him.

Out of all of the humans, one person living with his heart in unity with Him was enough for God to keep risking everything. Just one person! From the one would then come the family. From the family would then come the generations. To God, we are worth the risk.

God knew all of this when He created us.

THE TWO TREES

Eden contained many trees and each of them was designed to reproduce and become a forest. In God's great design, the trees would form the lungs of our world, as they would produce the oxygen that we breathe. There's an activation that I get people to do when they're learning to use their imagination in hearing the voice of God. They are to think of a tree that would describe them. When I'm doing this in a group, very rarely do I get people doubling up on a tree and thinking of the same one. It emphasizes the person's uniqueness and shows something of their identity. I help them unpack what part of the uniqueness of their tree speaks to their own identity. If someone says their imagined tree is a weeping willow, I will then ask whether they help people walk through times of sadness and grief. If they tell me that they connect with an Australian gum tree, I'll ask them about their connection to Australia and their ability to thrive in difficulty. I have found there's something so connected between creation and our identity. Through this activation, I love to help people see their identity through their connection with creation.

However, there are two trees in Eden that people rarely, if ever, align with: The Tree of Knowledge of Good and Evil, and the Tree of Life. From the way I read Genesis 2, it would seem to indicate that these are stand-alone trees. Maybe they were seedless. Maybe there was only ever going to be one of each. Even the thought of the fruit of these trees carrying seeds has my mind wondering what it would be to have a forest of either of these trees. (I may digress, but I wonder how we have seedless watermelons today! I love to eat watermelon without having to pick through the seeds, but, oddly, I'm eating a fruit without seeds.)

We know from Genesis 2 that those two trees were in Eden, and the only communication about them we have is that if Adam and Eve ate from the Tree of Knowledge of Good and Evil they were sure to die. But what do these two trees represent? What would happen when we entertained eating either of the fruits from these trees?

If we weren't to eat the fruit of the Tree of Knowledge of Good and Evil, would that mean that the fruit would just fall and rot on the ground? Would the animals be allowed to eat it, and what would happen if they did? I know that these questions are speculative at best. However, to hear the questions allows us to see that there are many things that we speculate on when we're trying to understand all that God has done in history. Each of our questions is healthy and needs to be asked. From what I know of God, He loves questions, and often I'm blown away by the answers. However, there are times when I've still got more questions and this tree seems to keep providing them to me. I wonder whether this is part of the seduction of this tree. The less we know, the more we want to know.

Whenever I'm walking through the bush (as we like to call it here in Australia), I will often come across mushrooms and berries. But I would have to be extremely hungry to entertain the idea of eating any of them. I love mushrooms, but I have no skill in knowing which ones are safe to eat. The only ones that I do eat are from a store. I am trusting that whoever grew them knew a lot more about them than I do. The fear I have in picking and eating them while on one of my walks is usually connected to my desire to not get violently ill, or even die! There are enough warnings out there about this for me to take notice and walk past them.

Then I wondered if God called this tree something else, would it then be less attractive to me. Most people who know me, know that I have an extreme dislike for zucchini. I can't stand them. People tell me that they're tasteless and that it's ridiculous that I have this aversion. They have tried to convert me with their recipes of zucchini greatness, but I won't be swayed. I only have to be told that zucchini is in the recipe and my stomach decides it is no longer hungry at all, regardless of whether you can taste it or not. There's something about the name of this vegetable that causes this reaction.

So I started wondering about the name of the tree, and why this tree was so attractive. What was it about the knowledge of good and evil that made it a fruit that was off-limits? Then it dawned on me that for one of us to think we can know all things that are good and evil elevates us to a judge and removes our ability to be in a relationship. You see, any time you judge someone, you are lifting yourself above them, thinking that you know all the details to then render a judgment of what is good and what is evil.

In the Bible, what is created by God is known as *good*. For example, when God created, He saw what He created was "good." By its very definition, there is nothing bad in it. You only have to look at a new-born child and see the *goodness* in that human. Or to stand on top of a mountain and look out on pristine beauty to see the *goodness* of His creation. We often hear people, and Jesus, declare "God is good." We can see that this "goodness" is more about what He has done than the part of creation you might be looking at. Evil is not just about what is bad or wrong, but is most often connected with Satan, the demonic, and anything that will tempt you away from God. It is the opposite of all the goodness that God has created. So, we are not merely talking about the difference between right and wrong, we are talking about understanding the difference between God and Satan.

Then, you might say, "Isn't this a good thing to know?", or "Why would God want to withhold this from us?" That's the very question that Satan landed on Eve, and I'll attempt to answer that in a later chapter. But again, the questions are good and by asking them, you are praying a prayer that God will not ignore.

So why would God put a tree in a garden that would cause us to die if we ate from it? While I believe the answer lies strongly in the design of us clinging to God's words and believing that His words are life, I also have to believe that the freedom to choose was an even greater gift that God was bestowing on us.

Let me give you an example from the Bible. Job was a man known for his righteousness. What that means is that Job had a powerful relationship with God. His love for Him and desire to be in a relationship with Him transformed Job and empowered his life and decisions. Everyone could see it, including Satan. Much like with the snake that entered Eden, in Job's story the talking snake, Satan, entered Heaven and engaged in a conversation that took Job's life in an unexpected direction.

48

To read Job 1 and 2 is like watching an opening scene from Star Trek where everything goes wrong and the Enterprise is all but destroyed! Job loses his livestock, his home, and his children. Marauding tribes took all of his livestock and forces of nature took his sheep and his family. Thousands of years outside of this moment have us declaring it is not fair. But again, the very nature of us declaring that something is not fair means that we've been influenced more by knowledge than we have of life.

Then Job's wife turned on him. It seems that she mocked him about his faith and integrity. She was arguing that his circumstances had shown that his faith was meaningless. As a father, it's extremely difficult for me to place myself in Job's shoes and understand all that he experienced or the many questions he had for God.

But Job had not lost everything. He still had his friends to surround him. When they came, they sat for seven days with him and said nothing. The Bible says, "for they saw that his suffering was too great for words." When Job finally spoke, he released his pain and it flowed from him like a flood. So much so that his friends were offended by what he was saying about his life and his God. It's in the offence that their relationship shifted, and after seven days of silence came the days of judgment. They had sat with him in his pain, but they did not sit with him in his questions. For his friends, his questions sounded dangerously like heresy. So they then delivered judgment after judgment to get him back to a better place. What were they doing? They were leading Job to the tree of knowledge of good and evil. They were attempting to show him how good God is and how evil Job was. There was only going to be death at the end of this conversation. Condemnation does not bring life. By its very definition, it leads to death. Job's friends were doing all that they knew how to do to convince Job that

God was correcting him and punishing him for his sin. They were, metaphorically, sitting under and eating from the wrong tree.

Long after Adam and Eve left Eden, the people of God were given the Law of Moses. This was a set of rules that would help them know the difference between good and evil. This, to me, shows that the people were no longer walking in a relationship with God, rather they were looking for the standard of living that God required. In Job's situation, it seems his three friends were very familiar with the Law but less familiar with the God the Law came from. They were very willing to weigh Job's life on a scale of judgment to find some flaw or hidden sin which would show why this had happened to him. They were so caught up in what they thought was right or wrong they failed to invite God into this conversation.

I know when I went through a season of breakdown in my life, the last thing I needed was for people to tell me how wrong I was and how punished I should be. I needed friends to not only sit with me in my pain but also my questions. Many people walked away from me in those moments. Who would want to be with a guy whose marriage had failed and ministry had come to a grinding halt? But in those moments, some stayed and others were drawn near to me. These are the ones who carried the very words of life, not phrases of condemnation. When they did this, it wasn't the tree of knowledge of good and evil that they led me to. It was to the Tree of Life, and it's the only tree that I want to be found under and eating of its fruit.

This tree could give eternal life, but it was not the fabled fountain of youth. Rather it was the tree that would invite us into eternity. As I said earlier, I believe this tree is now represented in Jesus. Eternity and righteousness are found in Him and He is now found in us. He

50

is the Tree of Life. This tree provided the supreme grace moment of creation. It was created to give eternal life to all who ate its fruit. In the same way, Jesus came to the earth so that all who received His message entered into eternal life. Which means, we don't have to try and find this tree to eat its fruit, we already have it. We no longer need to ask for it, as we already have tasted and seen that it is good. It is inherently a part of our design to eat from this tree. It carries a fruit that will always lead us to life. The very nature of its fruit leads away from death, condemnation, guilt, and shame.

Once I had a taste, I then discovered that Jesus was inviting me to feast! This is now our position, to sit at His table and feast on His goodness. You see, I believe that tasting and seeing is for tourists, but feasting is for families. When I travel, I can taste and see the various cultures that I engage with. But where I make my home is where I can feast. In Jesus, I have found my home and my feast. In the feast, I have discovered His eternity and His righteousness, and it is there that I have found life in all of its abundance.

But for Adam and Eve, the revelation of Jesus was a long way off, so they had the Tree of Life. They were freely allowed to eat from this tree. In fact, by God highlighting it, they were given intentional permission to take from it. Initially, nothing was stopping them from eating from it at any time they chose to do so. If anything was stopping them from eating, it was their own free will to do so. The only time they couldn't was when they chose to let go of the words that God had given them to cling to. But the tree did not ever stop doing what it was created to do: give eternal life.

The question that I leave you with is this: Which tree do you find yourself sitting under? If you are always consumed with what is right and wrong, whether you are clean or unclean, pleasing God or not pleasing Him, then I would simply invite you to think about sitting under a different tree. It's not about right and wrong, it's about life in all of its fullness. It's about loving God and the people around you without judgment and sharing the same grace you have found when you first metaphorically ate from what Jesus gave to you.

THE TALKING SNAKE

Genesis 3 introduces a new character into the narrative, a talking snake. If you've ever blamed your dog for eating your homework, then this story is probably where it all started. Genesis 3 is not the only time in the Bible that we hear Satan speaking, but it is the first, and it will give us an understanding of his character and behaviours.

Each of us will have these *talking snakes* in our lives. They are the voices that continue to attack our identity. They will try to convince us that we aren't who we think we are by telling us we aren't enough. They will remind us of past failures that seem to point to us being less than who God says we are.

Even as I'm writing this, last night I had a moment where a talking snake became a voice in my life. One of the things my wife and I love to do is sit around a fire pit enjoying the warmth of the fire and our relationship. The previous evening we had done this, so I cleared the coals from the night before. I poured them out near my back fence and noticed that there was still some smouldering, but in a moment of poor choices, I chose to hope they went out. Well, suffice to say they didn't. Hours after we had spent time around the fire pit we were sitting in our living room watching television when we heard an urgent knock at our front door. I opened it to be met with the news that my back fence was on fire! And sure enough, it was.

Long after putting the fire out and surveying the damage, I was sitting alone and ruminating on my own poor choices and where they had led me to. There was no one to blame but myself. Blaming myself is something that I seem to have done well for most of my life! So it was a familiar place to be in and a familiar voice to listen to. "Once again I'd made a mess." "Once again I'd made more strife from a situation that should have been common sense." You can see where my mind went with this and it wasn't leading me to the place of my God-given identity. I was going in the complete opposite way. I was listening to the talking snake, allowing blame to quickly become shame for me.

In Eve's case, the snake was using dangerous language that had her questioning the very words of God. God had told Adam that there was only one tree in Eden that they weren't to eat from and that was the Tree of Knowledge of Good and Evil. Everything else was freely available to them and it all tasted good. Sometimes it's what we can't have that seems to taste better in our minds. Maybe this was the case for Eve. Maybe Satan was assuming this for Eve as well. We know from the book of Revelation that pride was Satan's issue in Heaven. He too coveted the place that God occupied. He too imagined that what he couldn't have was better than what he had. So when he slithered up beside Eve that day he was probably speaking the same language that he spoke to himself long ago in Heaven.

In my experience, Satan always loves to work in half-truths and doubt. One of the greatest strategies of Satan is to distract us from what we're focused on. Adam and Eve were invited to tend and enjoy the garden. However, the one tree they were to tend without enjoying its fruit became the focus of their story. So Satan spoke to Eve of the reason God would withhold this fruit from her and how her life would be better off if she tried it. All it would take is a bite. He invited her to taste this tree and see its goodness as well. It seems as though it did taste good too, as she invited Adam to eat it as well. The distraction came powerfully when Satan convinced her that she would become like God if she ate it. She had walked with God through Eden and she knew of His love and presence. She only had to look around and see how magnificent Eden was to understand God's creative power. It wouldn't be a big step to entertain the thought that she could be like Him in these ways. Maybe she reasoned that if this was the only thing withheld from her then this must be the missing link, and to eat the fruit would make it all come together for her. Maybe Adam felt the same way, as he was complicit in eating the same fruit.

Curiosity is a powerful part of our creation. Each of us has it and it aids us in growing, learning, and transforming. However, if we're listening to the talking snakes in our lives at the cost of the voice of God, then we are on a road that will lead us away from His heart and our relationship with Him.

In Matthew 4, Jesus had His encounter with a talking snake, except this time it did not manifest as a snake; Satan can't hide from Jesus. However, he came with a very familiar series of half-truths and distractions. In Matthew 3 we read of the incredible moment of Jesus' baptism and of the way the Holy Spirit manifested as a dove while His Father spoke over Him with a booming voice, "This is my dearly loved Son, who brings me great joy" (Matt 3:17). So this is the context of Matthew 4 and you're able to see how quickly Satan will attempt to distract you from what God has just said.

After Jesus' baptism, He was led out to the wilderness by the Holy Spirit. While there He fasted and was tested. At the end of forty days Satan then turned up with a series of challenges, but he starts with the phrase, "If you are the Son of God..." Remember what the voice of God spoke over Jesus just weeks prior to this, "This is my dearly loved Son." So Satan goes straight after Jesus' identity. The concept of the word *if* is one that seems to be foremost in Satan's language. The very word can seed doubt, and if we're not secure in who we are, then it becomes a word that can change the course of our lives.

So Jesus was given three challenges by Satan, all commencing with the word *if*. The challenges went beyond the word *if*, they went into Jesus' circumstances. Satan wanted to lead Jesus to the place where he's doubting His identity and choosing to live a life that is not of God's design. Jesus had not eaten for 40 days, so obviously He was hungry. So Satan invited Jesus to use His creative powers and turn a stone into bread. Interesting to note that Satan was fully aware that the Son of God could do this. So he rolled the dice and risked it. Now, if you've read this story you will know that Jesus did not give Satan a conversation, He gave him a Bible study. Satan will always try to have you second-guessing what God is saying or doing. Jesus simply showed that He held more to God's words than any words that Satan could speak.

So to the challenge to satisfy His hunger by turning stone to bread, Jesus simply responded with, "People do not live by bread alone, but by every word that comes from the mouth of God" (Matt 4:4). Jesus might be hungry, but he's not hungry enough to start eating from the wrong source. In the next challenge, Satan took Jesus up and showed Him all the kingdoms of the world. In an attempt to steal Jesus' identity, Satan offered them all to Him if He would just bow down and worship him. Again, Jesus invited him back to a Bible study when He said, "You must worship the Lord your God and serve only him" (Matt 4:10).

Obviously Satan was not satisfied with the answer, so he tried to test Jesus again. He took Jesus to the top of the temple and invited Him to jump off. You can see where Satan's heading with this: if he could kill Jesus at his suggestion, then this would be the moment of Jesus eating from the wrong tree in Eden as well. Satan invited Him to command angels to come from Heaven to protect Him. Truth be told, Jesus could have, but again Jesus opened the Bible and led Satan back to God's words, "You must not test the Lord your God" (Matt 4:7). With the Bible study complete Satan exited the narrative. We then read that the very angels Jesus could have called on to save Him were there all along and they ministered to Him.

The strength of the attack was real and pointed at Jesus' identity. When I'm doing deliverance ministry I will often say to the person I'm serving, "You will always know a demonic attack if it's aimed at where you are strongest." This usually surprises the person as we have been taught for generations that Satan loves to attack us where we are weakest. However, in my experience this is not the case. Paul tells us very clearly that when he was at his weakest, God was at His strongest. So we can trust our weaknesses to God and His strength, and then focus on what's at stake when Satan attempts to go after our strengths. Your strength is your design. It is who God made you perfectly. He declared that you were good long before you were even conceived. He knew what He was doing when He formed you and He knew what

His love could accomplish through you. He didn't set you up to fail. He created you to live a life of fullness and relationship. He wrote His Word on your heart and planted eternity within you. He knew what He was doing as He formed you and sealed you with His Holy Spirit. And this is where Satan will try to plant seeds of doubt. He did it with Eve and he tried to do it with Jesus. He is not creative and will try to do it with us too.

With Eve, Satan tried to twist God's words when he said to her, "Did God really say you must not eat the fruit from any of the trees in the garden?" (Gen 3:1). He probably knew what God had said, but distraction is one of his mechanisms for sowing doubt. Eve's problem was that she began to reason with him and not just invite him to a Bible study like Jesus did. She should have clung to God's words, instead she started challenging them. Here's the thing, God doesn't mind us questioning His words, He just wants to be the one you have the conversation with.

Eve started reasoning with the talking snake when she said, "Of course we may eat fruit from the trees in the garden. It's only the fruit from the tree in the middle of the garden that we are not allowed to eat because God said, 'You must not eat it or even touch it; if you do, you will die'" (Gen 3:2–3). If you read Genesis 2, you will notice that the words He gave to Adam were slightly different to Eve's comment. To Adam God spoke of not being allowed to eat it. Eve added they were not allowed to even touch it. Had Adam said that to Eve? We don't know. This may be a side issue, but to me this is the first instance of religion creeping into Eden. When we create rules to keep us from breaking God's Word we have shifted from a relationship that is based on love to a contract that is based on law. I can understand the thinking behind it—if she didn't even touch it, she wouldn't be as tempted to eat it. History shows us that any time we try to do what God says by creating a rule system around obedience to Him we have exited Eden and decided to create human understandings and religion about how we connect with God.

Eve knew the outcome of her actions, but she didn't understand what Satan was trying to do when she started reasoning with him. After the eating of the fruit Satan went quiet. His job was done. He could stand back and watch the effects of when humans give in to his voice and allow his seeds of doubt to find their home in our hearts.

Every one of us deals with these talking snakes in our lives. We can use an activation here to help us understand how to deal with them. If you're unfamiliar with the language of *activation*, let me explain to you what I mean by it. God has given you an imagination to use and we do so every day of our lives. When you think of what you could do today, your mind will often play out pictures of what that could be. If you want to go to the beach, your imagination may give you a picture of that. We use it all the time.

We also use it when we pray. If I was sitting with you and asked you to pray, your mind would start constructing words that would make sense depending on what you're praying for. Once you've run out of words you will usually finish off the classic way of saying, "Amen." So, what would it look like if I asked you to pray, but instead of looking or listening for words, you looked for pictures?

One of the activations that I often lead is to imagine this snake as the words that it often loves to speak into your life to create doubt. I invite them to engage with those words with the words that God has either given directly to them or He's given historically in scripture.

Each time we're not reasoning with him, but simply showing him that we value God's words more. So once the lie, the half-truth, or the distraction has been seen, then we are given a beautiful opening to understand our identity and strength.

Quite simply, we are given a direction from God as to what we are to do with these talking snakes: we are to tread on them. In doing the above activation, I'm inviting the person to do this very act. Then each time they hear that familiar voice that is trying to sow seeds of doubt into their identity, they are able to tread on the snake and not reason with it. As you could see in Matthew 4, Satan isn't the most patient of creatures; he will tire and he will look for other opportunities to do the same again. Can I encourage you to find a group of people whom you trust to champion your identity and love you enough to keep you aware of the talking snakes on your journey?

CLOSING EDEN & THE PROBLEM OF SHAME

So the talking snake won a victory the moment Eve touched the fruit from the Tree of Knowledge of Good and Evil. In her mind, she had created a rule system around this tree and by touching it she was breaking her own rules. Events would then start unravelling around her that would end with her and Adam sowing fig leaves together and hiding from God at the time that they would be normally walking and talking with Him.

Shame is what the Bible says they were suffering. It's also something that Satan loves to lead us to and ensure that we live our lives from. How many of us can remember the most shameful moments of our lives as if they happened yesterday? I sure can and there are many times that I am reminded of what I have done wrong and of how I don't deserve to be in the place that I am.

Shame is a feeling that we need to process and not pack down. It has the power to attack our design and our identity. It has the power to change the course of our lives if we let it. For Adam and Eve, it sure did this. You see shame, at its core, corrupts how we see ourselves. We no longer look at ourselves as created in the very image of God, but as unclean or unworthy. Its voice will convince you that you are no longer seen or known for who God says you are. You are now known for what you have done wrong and that you can't change the past. It will ignore grace and mercy altogether. It will create a language of judgment and condemnation. It destroys relationships and has us walking away from the very people that God has placed around us.

If Jesus had succumbed to the temptations of Satan in Matthew 4, we would have most likely read of Jesus' journey through shame as well. So to unpack a little of the difference in their lives might help us understand how to deal with our shame. Adam, Eve and Jesus were all created uniquely by God. We all are created uniquely, and I'll get to that. But for this understanding see if you can follow what I'm saying. Paul calls Adam the first Adam and Jesus the last. He taught that sin gained an entry into the world through Adam and is finished through the life and death of Jesus. Sin's power gained ground through the shame that Adam and Eve hosted. However, sin's power was defeated by the life of one who never operated from the place of shame. Adam and Eve's curiosity of what the fruit of the Tree of Knowledge of Good and Evil did, outweighed the enjoyment of what the fruit from the Tree of Life gave. In my opinion, the Tree of Life was the physical manifestation of Jesus in Eden. Simply because eternal life flows from all who would eat of it. When Jesus invited the disciples to eat of Him in John 6, I believe He was saying what you're eating will give you eternal life.

Shame tried to bring an end to Adam and Eve's story right there and then. It tried to hide them away and close them down. The Bible says that they were even ashamed of their nakedness. Shame had them seeing that even God's creation needed to be hidden. Everything about shame works against our design. Feeling seen and known by others is a basic human need. The narrative of Eden shows us how far shame took Adam and Eve out of their relationship with God. They feared being seen. They feared being discovered for doing what they knew to be wrong. They feared punishment and, possibly for the very first time in humanity, they feared death. So they covered themselves up and hid.

If you know the story, you will know that blame became the language of shame. Adam blamed Eve and Eve blamed the snake. They didn't deny what they had done, they simply attempted to do to God what Satan had done to them; they tried to distract Him.

Have you ever wondered what would have happened if Adam and Eve just had asked for forgiveness right there and then? I know we'll only get that answer when we get to Heaven, but I do believe that God is the same yesterday, today, and forever. So I must believe that He is all about us choosing Him and choosing restoration. It then makes me wonder about the strength of shame and how it had Adam and Eve choosing a lesser form of relationship with God.

Let me share about my journey into and out of shame. At the age of 38, I was 5 years into full-time ministry and one year into my role as senior pastor. On the outside everything was great. My ministry was thriving, my family was growing and people were coming to faith every single week. On the inside, everything could not have been worse, my marriage was falling apart. I'd gotten married when I was 20 and had always believed that marriage was for life, but 18 years later I was looking at the despair and hopelessness that defined what my marriage looked like. I was a workaholic and insecure. Everything I did, every relationship that I formed was done to protect my very insecure heart. I didn't know who I was and I looked for those answers in others, rather than with my wife.

When it all came crashing down, my church stood me down for six months to work on my marriage and get my life back together. I sat with a counsellor every week for 6 months, and then every two weeks for the rest of the year. I got the opportunity to unpack why I did the things that I did; why I was led to do relationships with the people I chose and then finally what it looked like to be in a relationship with my wife. I came to the understanding that I had been living a life of desperately trying to please my earthly dad and not my heavenly One. I came to the understanding that I'd walked out on my marriage and subsequently my role as father to my kids. For the first six months of that year, I found myself, like Adam and Eve, hiding and desperately trying to cover my shame.

I knew what I had done. I knew the decisions that I made and how wrong I was. Just before all of this unravelled I had started praying a prayer, "God, judge me." It's not a prayer that I would encourage anyone to pray now, but at the time it was what I felt needed to happen. I couldn't keep living life that way. The journey that I embarked on, now that I look back, was one in which I could see God coming into Eden looking for me. He didn't create me to live in shame. He created me to be free. I realised I could not do this on my own or in my strength. God started bringing people into my life that would call me out of my shame.

The first was my wife, Trish. It would take a whole book to speak of the way that she loved me through that time, but the words that continue to ring in my spirit are, "I forgive you." The power of those words was more than I could bear. That one moment has been one of the most powerful moments of my life. When she spoke, "I forgive you," it changed my life. The second person was my counsellor. She is an amazing person who knows how to speak tough love into me. She said, "If you are willing, you will learn more in the next 12 months about your life than you will in the next 10 years." The last was a guy whom I met as a lawyer, who is now a great friend of mine. I sat in his office and through a lot of tears spilled out my story. At the end of it all I looked up at him and he said, "I can help you." These three people were Jesus in the flesh to me. When I combined the phrases of the three I found the words that called me out of hiding: "I forgive you, if you are willing, I can help you."

I don't know what phrase called Adam and Eve out of hiding, but I know that it would have been spoken in love. I imagine God's heart would have been aching as He spoke it. We have a God who will not let us stay hidden. Playing hide and seek with our creator is not a fair game, He knows where we are. The problem for Adam and Eve was that they didn't know where they were with each other, or with God. Choices were made to disobey God. Choices were made to listen to a talking snake. Choices were made to blame others for their own failings. We all know choices change things. We've all had moments when our choices have improved our lives and when they have not. Adam and Eve made a series of choices that weren't helpful for their own hearts, their marriage, and their relationship with their Creator. These choices then needed to be confronted and dealt with.

There's a part of me that just wanted God to fix their choices, to let them know that they'd done the wrong thing and send them back into Eden to keep being fruitful and multiplying. But, as we know, that's not what happened. The only one who could heal this was Jesus, and He was a few thousand years away from being born. He came to undo the effects of shame if we are prepared to trust in the very work that He has done. Adam and Eve, needed to trust in the work that God was doing that would finally be fulfilled in Jesus.

There's a question that's been bugging my understanding of grace in this story and of why Eden needed to be closed to Adam and Eve. The problem with disobedience is that when you do something once, it's easier to do it again. The Tree of Knowledge of Good and Evil was still there in Eden, as was the Tree of Life. Could they have moved between trees each time that they were tempted to eat from the wrong tree? Would the Tree of Life become their fix to the solution of shame? Could they bypass a relationship with God altogether by simply eating the fruit that came from the Tree of Life? If the history of humanity is anything to go by, then I think yes! We seem to gravitate to the path of least resistance, and the fruit of Tree of Life could have become what they believed in, rather than the One who created them. It was never God's plan to destroy either of these trees. Rather, it seemed that He planned to teach them about the relationship that would one day lead them back to Eden, where they would know the wonder of the relationship that He was offering them. So, they lost Eden. What they didn't lose was their relationship with God. It wasn't the same as what they had, but it wasn't gone.

He had not stopped being present with them or protecting them, and the ground would still provide for them. However, they were now learning to deal with emotions that they had never had to deal with. The perfect environment of Eden, which was physical, emotional, and spiritual, had been upset by the internal emotions of fear, shame, and guilt. Romantically, we would love God to hit some kind of divine reset

66

that has Adam and Eve forgetting their past and still in Eden. Often, I still hear Christians saying this today for their own lives as if their past choices have not affected them, or those around them, in any way. The truth is that they do affect us and others. For God to heal us from past poor choices, He needs to lead us into a journey of discovery. Adam and Eve's journey of discovery was an act of grace, not an act of condemnation. Condemnation would have destroyed them at the moment. Condemnation would have had them wandering alone. It was grace that found them, and grace that didn't let them stay hidden. It was grace that provided for them and continued to protect them. Lessons needed to be learned from the mistakes of their past. Through learning from these mistakes, they were able to pass on generationally what had brought them to those choices. They also were able to give witness of the God that continued to lead them from those choices and back into life with Him.

So, *if the Bible shows us that God still had a relationship with us, what was lost in Eden?* God created us with the ability and freedom to make choices. In the moment where they chose to eat from the wrong tree, Adam and Eve were making choices for their life based on their wisdom, rather than God's. They lost the purity of the intimacy that was held within a relationship that was founded in pure love. The relationship they were given found nothing withheld from them, they were entrusted with all creation. However, their choices broke the trust which allowed their guilt and shame to create a narrative of fear that drove them away from the One who loved them. Think of your own relationships when trust was broken and fear became the narrative. You were no longer operating from the design of the original relationship blueprint. If we listen to the fear of punishment, we find that shame becomes our hiding place. We lose our identity, as shame will convince us that we are unworthy of the safe relationship that we thought we had in the first place. So, the relationship is still there but it is no longer operating like it used to. Healing is needed that directly deals with what caused the guilt and shame in the first place. Healing doesn't just happen. There needs to be a healer who carries love to see past the offence to the heart for an opportunity for healing. Then a beautiful thing happens: love becomes the narrative of the relationship. When a person is loved and given the opportunity to be released from their shame, hope grows. When love and hope combine, then trust or faith grows. It is the same with the original design of our relationship with God. It is still there, but there needs to be a healer that carries with them a narrative of restoration and healing. Faith, hope, and love are, and always will be, the great hallmarks of a restored relationship with Him.

So, if we were still able to have a relationship with God before Jesus died for us, then why did He have to die? This is a brilliant question and one that many believers shy away from. Here's my take on it: Forgiveness always needed a sacrifice. It was modeled in the Law of Moses, but it was fulfilled in the death of Jesus. But *He didn't die on the cross so that we could have a relationship with Him—we already had that. He died on the cross so that guilt and shame could no longer control that relationship.* The very thing that had us hiding has now been dealt with. Now we meet Him forgiven. It was God's way of revealing His great love to humanity. It was His great plan to, once again, give us complete access to the Tree of Life, the Garden of Eden, and rediscover the freedom Adam and Eve had. Guilt and shame no longer keep us from those. God has forgiven us, and has invited us back into those deep places of intimacy with Him. Jesus' stories in Luke of the Great Feasts give us an understanding of the level of restoration that He has invited us all into.

Whenever you think about a feast, I can guarantee you that your imagination won't stop at an empty table! Each time I've asked someone to imagine a feast, usually the imagery reveals so much food on the table there is no place for the plates! If this is in your imagination then be encouraged that the abundance of Heaven is speaking to you right now! In Jesus' story of preparing a feast, the master had his servants send out invites to all his friends. When the feast was ready, he sent out his servant to get those friends to come to the table. However, the only thing that the servants came back with was excuses as to why they couldn't attend the feast. This upset the master, but it didn't stop the feast! If anything, it revealed the master's desire to share the abundance of his table. In Luke 14:23, Jesus said, "Go out into the country lanes and behind the hedges and urge anyone you find to come, so that the house will be full." I love how Jesus speaks of those "behind the hedges." Jesus was inviting even those that were hiding to come to the feast!

I believe that this was what happened to Adam and Eve—God invited them to come out of hiding. It's a biblical theme that hedges are what God builds to protect us, but often it's our guilt and shame that has us building hedges to protect ourselves from condemnation and shame. Jesus' great sacrifice brought about this brilliant moment where His love invited us to come away from hiding and to stop protecting ourselves from the shame within our lives. It was His great way of saying to us that there is now no condemnation for us. Quite simply, there is nothing now to fear from God.

As brilliant as this is, there is something we need to be aware of. As He has given us access to Eden, there is still access to the Tree of Knowledge of Good and Evil. That tree is still there. This means we can still go to that place where our wisdom will be sought over God's wisdom. The unbelieving world will dismiss this as a fairy-tale, but those of us who believe in God for who He says He is will have a completely different view. It doesn't take a genius to look at the state of humanity and question whether following our wisdom could ever lead us back to Eden. However, humanity seems to keep making the same mistakes. We keep looking to anyone else other than God. I believe that humanity does this because we have been generationally convinced that God is, at best, distant, or at worst, a fairy-tale.

Choosing to follow Him is choosing to listen to Him. In listening to Him, we find that we can trust Him. In trusting Him, we find that we are in love with Him as He is in love with us. Think about this for a moment: the people you trust the most are the ones that you love the most. The ones that you love are the ones that you generally listen to. It is the same with our relationship with God. Jesus' sacrifice gave the most profound statement of love. It is safe to return to Him and it has always been His design for this to happen. Nothing has separated us from God. King David discovered that he couldn't escape Him, nor can we. David discovered that we needed to have a renewed or clean heart to feel close with God, one that no longer was bound by fear, guilt or shame, one that was fully engaged with the very real relationship that God has invited us into. He stands at the gates of Eden and invites us into the very place of the original design with Him. Jesus said, "Seek the Kingdom of God above all else, and live righteously, and he will give you everything you need." (Matt 6:33). It's time to believe that this is no longer a fairy-tale, this is our reality.

Unbelief is the greatest challenger to this kind of thinking. Like I said earlier, when I read about the Apostle Paul, who felt he could walk boldly into the throne room of Heaven, it always challenged me. I've now realised that Paul had come to an understanding of the reality and magnitude of what Jesus' sacrifice had given him. He no longer needed to hide. His shame was only being held there by his resolutions, not by God's design. Jesus had given him forgiveness, restoration, and then transformation through grace. Without Jesus' sacrifice, this would have been some kind of fairy-tale. With Jesus' sacrifice, this was now a reality. Forgiveness, restoration and grace, are all a part of our divine design.

I find that our divine design is being challenged daily, mostly by our own beliefs of how a relationship with God operates. If we believe this relationship happens through effort on our part, then we trust in our strength. If we believe that it is to happen only in Heaven, then we have to wait for death. If we believe God wants to punish us for our disobedience, then we try relationship from a place of fear, or a place of a contract with Him. What would it look like if we believed our relationship with God could look like what Jesus modeled and it could affect our relationships with people around us? If we love as we have been loved by God? If we treat others as we would like to be treated? If we show compassion and grace as we have been? If we love those who hate us? If we forgive those who have harmed us or offended us? These are all the teachings of Jesus that He not only spoke but lived. Jesus is the perfect example of the life and relationship that we are invited to live in with God. No longer distant, no longer fearing being judged. No longer waiting for death, but living life to the fullest now in the present moment.

As I have said previously, this was powerfully modeled to me when my life went into crisis. Early on in my healing journey, I was asked to join a peer support group of seven other pastors for three years. Throughout that time, I was invited to be open and honest with my life. As a pastor, whose life went into crisis during ministry, this was the last thing that I thought my wounded heart needed. A marriage in crisis, the shame that I walked in, and the fear of condemnation that I carried were all screaming that grace was not something that I would find in a group like this. I kept coming up with every reason not to go. The only reason I agreed to be a part of this group was because of the grace of the one who invited me into it. He was the same person who said, "I can help you." His love and grace for me went beyond any "contract" of relationship. There was nothing cheap about what he did for me. He counted a cost to stand beside me, and here he was again offering me a road back to Eden.

This group would spend a week away together, each year for three years. Each person was given all the time needed to share their story during the week. So the first week away, one of the leaders went first and shared his story. It was deep and spoke of the challenges of his life and also the joys. At the end of his sharing, he then invited people to ask questions. As I listened to the questions that were being asked, I soon realised there was nothing shallow about what was happening. These weren't simple questions that you could sidestep with a cute metaphor. These guys were there ready to listen to the tangible answers that flowed from this man's heart! When he finished, he then asked who wanted to go next. By that stage, my anxiety was enormous and I knew that I didn't want to wait another moment. This was my moment. For the next two hours, my story poured from my heart and tears poured from my eyes. I shared the failures that had become so much of my life. I shared the journey into it, and then from where my healing was starting to flow. It was so raw, and I allowed myself to be vulnerable. When I finished there was silence, and for a few moments I thought that I had been wrong to put myself in that position. I thought I'd overshared. It was then that the miracle of grace occurred.

Most of these men I barely knew before this week, but then every one of them gathered around me. Instead of condemnation, came love. Instead of judgment, I felt healing. One of the greatest gifts of my life was given in the most vulnerable time of my life. God had led me there to show me the gift of grace that He'd already given me, and He was using His followers to demonstrate it. To this day, every one of those men is still in my life. Each time we catch up, we speak from the heart and to each other's hearts. When we are in crisis, we know that God has given us a relationship to stand together through it all.

Shame has a very powerful way of closing down relationships. It didn't take Adam and Eve long to understand how shame worked. It had them hiding, and it had them blaming. Quickly they learned what it was to be right and wrong. Neither of them liked being wrong, and they both tried to defend themselves. When God turned up for His walk with them in the cool of the evening, He came across a conversation that was out of rhythm with their design. A conversation that went in a direction other than "I was wrong and I am sorry."

Adam and Eve were found hiding. In many cultures, shame will not let us look another person in the eye. I know in Australian culture that's a thing. If I find myself unable to make eye contact with a person, I know that there may be a problem in the relationship that needs addressing. Adam and Eve did what most of us do, they ran for cover and looked for a place of protection from the judgment that they thought was coming their way.

There are many stories in the Bible where shame was a dominating force. But it's the story of David and Bathsheba that gets me every time. It's probably because so much of David's behaviour and choices are ones that I could relate with. His shame was a major player in David's life. It controlled choices that had dire consequences for everyone involved. In 2 Samuel 11, we find that David was getting older and was no longer heading out with Israel's army to battle. He was spending his time in Jerusalem. One day he was on his palace verandah when he looked down and saw a beautiful woman bathing on her roof. Her name was Bathsheba. Instead of looking away, he continued to look down. Until finally his lust started speaking louder than common sense. He asked after her and found that she was married and that her husband was out with the army. Here's the moment that David should have looked up and not down. But, he sent for her, slept with her and got her pregnant.

His shame found him trying to hide his failure. In most nations, the king could do whatever he wanted. But in Israel, the king was under God like every other person in the Kingdom. The same rules applied to all. David had a lot of power and was trusted by many. So, he hatched a plan that would hopefully protect him from his failure and shame.

He called Bathsheba's husband, Urriah, back from the battlefield under the guise that he wanted a report of how the battle was going. Then David sent him home for a night with his wife. It sounded like a safe plan. It had all the markers of being able to cover his failure, but for one thing... Urriah was a man of honour and he refused to go home and spend time with his wife while the army was out fighting and sleeping in the fields. He slept in the guards' quarters at the palace. David, not to be deterred, decided that the next night he would get him drunk and then surely he would go home and sleep with his wife. But again, Urriah would not go home. Finally, David wrote a command, sealed it, and gave it to Urriah to give to Joab, the leader of the army. In his own hands, Urriah unknowingly carried his death warrant. The order was to send Urriah out where the fighting was fiercest and then at an opportune time, pull the men back and let Urriah be killed. Which is exactly what happened.

Your shame has a way of affecting every relationship that surrounds you. It affected Bathsheba; she was pregnant and now mourning the loss of her husband. It affected Urriah; he was murdered. It must have affected Joab, as he would have known his order was to make sure Urriah died looking like a casualty of war. It affected David, as he became a murderer. Then it affected the entire nation. David's shame was controlling the hand of the king. It had led him to the Tree of Knowledge of Good and Evil, where he sat. He had tasted its fruit and knew that his life had been changed. His shame would have messed with his relationship with God for his part. I have found that when my shame pops up, I second guess what God is speaking. It's like trying to carry on two simultaneous conversations, one with God and one with myself. On one hand, I love God's voice and want to encounter the love that flows from Him. But on the other hand, I'm wondering if my failures have damaged my relationship with Him, and what else will be damaged as a result. A part of me is hoping that God will just ignore it and hopefully everything will be good. Then another part of me just wants to get it over with and lance the boil that my actions have created. It's in those moments that it feels like Eden is closed and the Tree of Life is outside of my reach. But it's not true, it's an effect of my shame.

Psalm 51 is commonly known as David's great psalm of confession about this moment of failure. Here we see a man who was in turmoil and did not know what to do with his shame. He knew what he had lost. He had walked with God in the cool of the evening, listened to His plans, and had conversations. He knew the joy that he once lived his life in, and he knew it had been replaced with deep sorrow.

In 2 Samuel 12, David was confronted by the prophet Nathan. God had told Nathan what David had done. David was about to learn there was no place that he could go to hide from God. God was not doing this to bring him further shame, but to bring him out of shame and into the light again. God didn't come in and change his circumstances and realign his life. There was a journey of restoration that David would have to go through, and part of that was dealing with the consequences of his actions. For the relationships around him to be restored, and him to be set free, he needed to be present in the conversations and face his consequences.

Remember, Jesus came to seek and save that which was lost (Luke 19:10). Long before Jesus was born, God was doing the same thing here for David. God's forgiveness was given to David, but forgiveness did not mean that his past failures had gone. Forgiveness was an opportunity for him to find healing from the very beliefs that trapped him and had him feeling shame in the first place. The brilliance that I have found with forgiveness and grace, is that the more that I give it, the more I receive it. It is so much more powerful to enter into a relationship knowing that grace is the foundation. When this is the case, we do not come with a "contract" of rights and wrongs, we come with the attitude of love and acceptance. Our relationship will not be based upon good or bad deeds but on mutual grace and acceptance. This is what Jesus came to give each of us, an intimate relationship. He came to remove every obstacle so that this relationship could be given freely; not cheaply.

There's a phrase that's been spread around called *cheap grace*. It is usually used when people assume that we are ignoring the poor behaviour and consequences of the past, with no need for a relationship or discipleship journey. Grace is only cheap if we give nothing to the person, other than words. Jesus didn't come to the world, just to give us God's words. He came to give us God's love. He came to love us as God loves Him. Let me explain. If someone comes and asks for forgiveness of me, and I say, "I forgive you," then walk away, where does that leave the person? Most likely, we will be out of relationship. The grace that I've offered has cost me very little. In fact, I would call it cheap. For me, God's grace and love are a part of the same understanding. His love and grace is His investment into my life. Every part of it, designed to draw me closer to Him and designed to heal, restore, and transform me. There is no greater investment that you can place in a person than to invest with love and grace. A relationship where these are the primary character traits will be stronger and more trusted.

So, when someone asks me to forgive them, this is a profound moment where the relationship can become stronger. At that moment, the person has humbled themselves and asked you back into a relationship with them. They are vulnerable, and they are inviting you to restore something that you have the power to restore. It is then that you get to decide how much you will invest. Will it be cheap, or will it be given freely. If it's *cheap*, it will come with conditions of behaviour. If it's *given freely*, it will come with a desire for restoration. That may not mean immediately, and there may need to be many issues worked through or considered. (Dangerous relationships must be considered differently. I am not suggesting you put yourself in danger.) However, the destination for the healthy, non-abusive relationship is one in which restoration is in the journey. I believe that if grace is a feature of my story, then restoration will be found throughout my story.

The closing of Eden started the plan of God for its grand re-opening, which no one expected. What followed was thousands of years of waiting, listening, and prophesying. One prophecy was added to the next and gave somewhat of a clearer picture from the last one. But at the same time, it wasn't clear enough for anyone to put the whole picture together. They knew that God was sending a Saviour. However, as the years continued, the people of God grew impatient and began to form a person in their imaginations that would release them from bondage and deliver them to their Promised Land. But the promised land that God was planning was not bound by physical borders. To do so would mean that one country could claim ownership of God again. It would be more like what Jesus spoke to the Samaritan woman in John 4; it would not matter where we went to worship, but who we went to worship.

Jesus' death continued the plan of God to bring this to fulfilment. When He died, the Bible records that an earthquake occurred simultaneously. As the earth shook, the curtain in the temple that separated the Holy of Holies from the people was torn in two. To a non-believer that may have been a curious coincidence. But to the believer, the tearing of that curtain spoke of a door being opened that no one could close again. A moment when nothing separated us from God anymore and all of us were able to boldly enter into that Holy place.

Previously, once a year the High Priest of the Jews would cleanse himself and enter into the Holy of holies to minister to God. A rope was tied around one of his ankles and he wore a bell, so if he died the bell would stop ringing and they would know to drag him out. This protected them from violating the Jewish law forbidding anyone else from entering the Holy of holies. It was holy and only those chosen and cleansed could enter. With the huge dividing curtain torn open by Jesus' sacrifice releasing us from the power of sin and death, we were invited to encounter the very presence of God. God broke out of the Holy of holies and was made available to us all.

Some might say, "So what? What does it all mean?" Your beliefs around encountering God will reveal what you know of God's character. For some, God may be considered distant, so they might believe they need to entreat Him to respond to them. For others, God may be considered to be close and they feel they have been changed by His love. There are as many different beliefs as there are people. However, it is clear that this is no longer a place to go physically, but spiritually and relationally. It's not a place to bring a sacrifice to please God, it's a positioning of your heart to love God.

If you believe that you need to meet with God out of some kind of duty that will result in Him being happy with you, you may not find what you expect. That sounds like religion, which is often our best guess at the way God works. This has little to do with the way the Bible has explained. We do not need to tick boxes to make sure that we have done all that we think we should to have a relationship with God. Again, this is not what any form of healthy connection and relationship looks like. Think of Jesus' story. So many people healed, delivered, touched, loved, taught, shared a meal with, walked beside, resurrected, cared for, accepted, and graced upon. The gospels are a treasure trove of the investments of His love and life into others. This was no religion that was bound by what He must do, or was even commanded to do. This was a life of loving the people whom God brought to Him. Jesus lived from that metaphoric Holy of holies. He was showing us God's love from within Him. He didn't need to be in the temple, a church, or Bible college. He simply lived knowing that God lived within Him and that God's love flowed through Him. His very life opened Eden for us. He was the road that led us back into the Holies of holies, and into the Father's heart.

EDEN'S PATH BACK

Jesus taught on the difference between a narrow path and a crowded highway to destruction (Matt 7:13-14). In two short verses, He gave us an understanding of the road He invited us all to discover which would lead to eternal life. So, why hide it? Why not make Eden at the end of the wide road that no one could miss? Well here's a thing, I think He did.

The challenge that He faced in the first century was that He was starting from scratch. He was doing what no one expected or was willing to do. He was loving people into the Kingdom one person at a time. Any time you are pioneering a new thing, you begin to realize that few others are walking the path you have found.

The angel of the Lord prophesied a path that would usher in the new Kingdom to Zechariah. He said to him, "And you, my little son, will be called the prophet of the Most High because you will prepare the way for the Lord. You will tell his people how to find salvation through the forgiveness of their sins. Because of God's tender mercy, the morning light from heaven is about to break upon us, to give light to those who sit in darkness and the shadow of death, and to guide us to the path of peace" (Luke 1:76-79). Then Jesus spoke of the path when He quoted Isaiah, "The prophet Isaiah was speaking about John when he said, 'He is a voice shouting in the wilderness, 'Prepare the way for the Lord's coming! Clear the road for him!''" (Matt 3:3)

In these verses we discover the path back to Eden. The road that Isaiah prophesied is the road to Jesus, who is the way back to Eden. The prophecies were given hundreds of years before Jesus' birth. They would have been a source of theological debate for all of those years. But the day Jesus was born was the day the gate to the narrow path was thrown open, never to be closed again.

It may be controversial, but I believe that the wide road is religion and the narrow path is our personal relationships with God and others. Religious organisations and denominations speak to the masses, where relationship speaks to the heart of the person in front of us.

Long ago when Emperor Constantine made Christianity the religion of state, something shifted for churches. They no longer needed to be hidden. They could build structures and provide locations where people could go to learn about God. While this might have been liberating for the Christians of the time, years later we have adopted the process of teaching the masses rather than loving the people. Churches became places where morality and ethics could be taught en masse. In becoming a part of the church, you needed to agree with the teachings and theologies of that particular church. All along we were losing the personal relationship with God and starting to live through the leader of a church. We came to hear what they had to say, or what God had told them. We came to develop practices that would keep us from sinning or straying from what the church taught. To do so brought judgment, or even condemnation. We were beginning to be herded, rather than be the leader of our own choices and free will. It's far easier to move a lot of people down wide roads than narrow pathways.

In herding the many down the wide road we lost the understanding of the importance of people's stories and lives. We stopped listening to people. We started telling them what we thought they needed to hear, rather than being the ones who are willing to listen. The narrow way may have seemed less efficient in getting the gospel to the masses, but it has definitely had the most effectiveness.

Jesus had thousands of people gather around His ministry, but at His death, there were few. He chose to do life with twelve disciples and love each one of them into a place of relationship and understanding. These twelve were given a beautiful invitation through the narrow gate and its path. When we read of these men in church history, we see that each of them (other than Judas) clung to Jesus' words and life. They changed the world one individual encounter at a time. Jesus wasn't miserly in the invitations either. When five thousand people followed Him into the wilderness He sought to feed and teach them. Each word taught and each mouthful given was a powerful invitation to follow Him down a narrow path. To do so, however, meant they would have to give up the wide path that many were walking.

Each week the religious leaders would cite centuries-old teachings of living a pure and godly life. They would read scriptures that they had committed to memory. They had committed holy words to their minds, little did they know that God was far more interested in their hearts. So they led the masses by their minds and ignored the relationship which God had planned from the days of Eden to restore. So when Jesus showed up in the flesh their minds weren't able to comprehend what their hearts were feeling. For so long they had been blindly travelling down the wide road, not realising that God wasn't leading them along it. Long ago Moses refused to move along any road unless God went ahead of him. Now centuries later, God's people were being herded, like cattle, down a road that didn't lead them to a relationship with Him, but destruction.

Isaiah prophesied that John the Baptist would make the road and then clear the road so that others could find it. What do you think Isaiah meant when he said that John would "clear the road"? Were there things on it that would cause us to fall? What was it that Jesus introduced that caused the people such great difficulty to understand? People spoke of the authority that came from Jesus when He spoke. They marvelled at the prophecies that they had seen fulfilled. They were in awe of the miracles that He performed. But they were *changed* by the love that He expressed and they experienced.

Condemnation and shame did not come from Jesus' mouth, as it seemed to flow from the religious people. A woman could cry on His feet and anoint them with perfume without any concept of fear in doing so. A woman who was thrown at Jesus' feet, caught in the very act of adultery, walked away from Him forgiven and seen without shame. Jesus had disempowered condemnation with a few simple words. He had disempowered fear, simply by being present with this woman. Jesus walked to the possessed and set them free. He touched the lepers to heal them and was not afraid to catch what they had. He was willing to sit with Nicodemus and not bring judgment into the conversation. Jesus walked a different path; He called it "narrow." I think that more and more of us are finding it because we want to be loved and to love. We're no longer willing to listen to religious conversations that lead us to depend on the organised church for what Jesus has so freely given us.

This path might be narrow, but for the ones, like Nicodemus, who are asking some very big questions about faith, it's a path worth seeking. If they can't find it in churches, they will look for it elsewhere.

These are the days when the people with big questions are going to grow. People's lives are changing because of the choices they are making due to the questions they are asking.

I believe this is the life all of us are invited to live. When we, as the church, make up rules for how people travel the path, we mess with the design. If we mess with the design, the plan will be hard to see. It is Jesus who promises to add "all these things" to our lives. Maybe it's time we relaxed and let Him do what He says He will do.

UNDERSTANDING YOUR DESIGN

So let me help you understand something of your design. Jesus once said, "My nourishment comes from doing the will of God, who sent me, and from finishing his work" (John 4:34). I love the language of "nourishment" in "doing God's will." It tells me that in discovering and doing His will, a nourishment will grow within me. God's will for Jesus is as unique as God's will for you and me. The intention behind it is the same, but the time, location, and expression will be vastly different for each of us. I believe that Jesus had this in mind when He told us that we would do "greater things" (John 14:12, NIV) than He would.

One of the questions that I'm most asked is, "How do I know what God's plan, or will, is for my life?" Or I will hear people say, "I don't want to miss the plan that God has for my life." I believe that these are two thoughts that are seeded into our lives by God. Most people want to do something with their life that impacts others. But, they also don't want to waste their time following dreams that will never become reality. So, often they keep going around in circles, asking the same questions over and over. They end up doing very little with the time they have been given.

In a world that strives to succeed and to be seen, it comes as quite a surprise to understand that in God's eyes, you have already succeeded, and you are already seen. Slowing yourself down so that this truth becomes a reality is important. Slowing yourself down to understand the design of the Designer is a key of the Kingdom.

The plan for your life is a by-product of following the design of your life. If you don't follow God's design, you will be complaining about God's plan. If you don't follow the design, the plan will not achieve what was promised. So, "What am I designed to do?" Here's the design parameters that I believe God has given to us:

1. Love God with everything we have (Deut 6:5)
2. Love others, as we love ourselves (Lev 19:18)
3. Love others, as Jesus has loved us (John 13:34)

It sounds simple, and it is. We over complicate our lives with all kinds of mantras and habits, only to come back to the same place, asking the same questions of our design and plan. But it's all wrapped up in these three invitations of Jesus with the common denominator of *love*. If love is the common denominator, what does the process look like? Loving God with everything I've got can equate to Jesus saying, "seek first the Kingdom of God" (Matt 6:33). It's a brilliant statement, but I believe there is more to it than that. For me to "seek" tells me that there is more yet to discover. So, for me to "love God with everything I've got" is a relationship concept where I've learnt to walk with Him in every moment of my life. It is knowing that He is a good Father and knowing that the plans He has for me revolve around our relationship. For Jesus to say that He only does what He sees the Father doing (John 5:19) means that Jesus had a relationship that was based on family and presence; "I will only understand what God is doing if I understand that He is my Father and I can see the things He does." This has nothing to do with striving or earning that place. If we are family, we are born into it. We can rest in the knowledge that it's not what we are doing, but who we are.

Resting is part of the original design. If you don't learn to rest, then the plan may not cooperate with the change of design. Rest is even in the 10 commandments that God gave to the children of Israel! Not resting is like failing to put oil in an engine, and then expecting the engine to operate at the design specifications. It won't end well. Unless you correct this, the end result could be catastrophic for both the engine and your plans of getting to your destination.

What does *rest* look like? In Genesis 2, the Bible says that God "rested from all His work." When I ask people what that means, generally I get a blank face looking back at me, or they say, "He did nothing." I actually don't think that's the case. So what does rest look like to God? The word *rest* in Hebrew means "abode/home". When I discovered this I felt that I'd received one of the largest revelations of my life! When God rested, He made Himself at home! The next question that flowed through my mind was, "What does it look like for God to make Himself at home?" Straight away the revelation came that God did this by spending time in relationship with those He loved!

Resting and success, in our culture, seem to be competing voices. If we want to succeed, then we must work hard and long. For many years I have suffered at the hands of the fear of failure. It was this fear that constantly had me avoiding rest. I felt that I had to strive, work, or achieve to succeed in ministry and in life. But that led me to catastrophic failure. Like the engine with no oil, everything imploded and I was no closer to my goal. Rest, for me, is a word that reminds me of rhythm. As a musician I know the difference of being in and out of rhythm and I see this so clearly with rest. When I don't prioritise it in my life, the rhythm of my life starts going astray. I can see it, my wife can sense it, my family suffers for it and those I'm in relationship with wonder why I've gone quiet! Rest is often the first casualty in the striving to live a life that we love to call "full." However, rest is not an optional extra in this life, it is in our design and it needs to happen. Make yourself at home with some of those that God has placed in your life.

Sometimes He places people around you to love you as He has loved them, as much as He has placed you in their lives to love them as you love yourself. This is another inherent piece of our design. It is also another part of ensuring the plan works to the fullest. Like resting, I had to learn to love. Love is a concept that can be described, but for it to be learned it must be experienced. For it to be experienced there is always a risk involved. As God risked creating us, so we step out and risk being vulnerable and seen. From the days of creation, we have been called to understand this. But, for me, it seems that I kept making the same mistakes, and became hesitant to take the risks that I once did that would lead me into relationships with others.

Another important aspect of our design is grace. Again, very simple to say and sing. But if we leave it there, we get no closer to understanding the magnitude of this design feature of our lives. Grace cannot be understood unless it is understood through love. Grace and love cannot be separated spiritually, biblically, or presently. The plan thrives when these two great character traits of our King are given full permission to move through our lives. To give them this permission is to allow transformation to occur in our lives. The problem for many of us is that we put limitations or restrictions on the grace that has been so freely given to us. The ongoing effect that I have discovered when I put restrictions on grace was that my transformation was drip-fed rather than poured out. We pray and cry out for more of Him, but we fail to understand that He is already within us in fullness. He has given us the ability to love and demonstrate this very grace in fullness. You may have other aspects of your design that feature more heavily than rest, love, and grace. These are the three that God continues to encourage and challenge me into. Life is so busy that we can easily give up rest. Relationships are challenging, and risking the vulnerability to love at Jesus' level can be avoided. Grace has the brilliant ability to help us see people as Jesus sees them, but when we're tired and risk-averse to love, we can tend to think more about ourselves than those we are invited into a relationship with.

If you want to see God's plan for your life, then start with the design He has for your life. You will find the plan will be a by-product of the design. You will see God's hand guiding you and His love empowering you.

WALKING IN EDEN

The Bible is full of what I call "Eden Moments" of the Kingdom being here now and present. These are biblically recorded times when God was visible, verbal, and relational with people. Here are some of the testimonies and encounters with God. In these people's stories, it's easy to see their character and the character of God with each one.

JACOB

In Genesis 28, Jacob got to taste what it was like to once again walk in Eden. The Old Testament is littered with stories of God powerfully entering into people's lives, and Jacob's story was one of those. Everything else seemed to fade away when God entered the story. Abraham, Moses, Job, David, Jonah, and Ezekiel are all examples of what happens when you receive an encounter with God. They all got to taste what Adam and Eve had lived every day at the beginning of the Garden.

Jacob's "taste" happened when all the circumstances surrounding him were screaming that he was hunted, homeless, alone, abandoned, and penniless. We pick the story up in Genesis 27, where Jacob stole his brother's birthright. Birthrights don't mean a lot in our culture, but they did in Jacob's. The first-born son was traditionally seen as the family's priest (Num 3:12 & 8:18), and they were also given the double portion of the paternal inheritance (Deut 21:15-17). They were a means of passing on wealth and status, normally passed to the first-born son, which was his brother Esau. Jacob deceived his father to steal this from Esau. For a brief moment, he must have thought that he had gotten away with it. Until his brother, Esau, came looking for their father to receive the first-born blessing, as was his birthright! When the truth was discovered, everything changed and came crashing down for Jacob. Any time that you feel you need to steal something, the message your feelings are sending you is wrong.

Rachel, their mother, knew that Esau was angry enough to kill Jacob. She secretly sent Jacob back to where his ancestors came from. In Haran, his uncle, Laban, lived. Jacob had never met his uncle, but was now desperately hoping he would take him in. All thoughts of the first-born blessing must have seemed a thousand miles away.

However, it was in this journey that Jacob got a taste of Eden. Somewhere between home and Haran, Jacob went to sleep in a place that the next morning he named "Bethel." In his sleep, he dreamt a very famous dream. Heaven opened and a staircase came down. Angels were travelling up and down the staircase to Heaven. At the top of the staircase, stood the Lord and He spoke to Jacob in the dream. He gave to him the promises that He gave to his grandfather, Abraham. He promised him a home, a family, and security. He promised him all of this when his circumstances showed none of this.

I often wonder what my response would have been to a dream like this. Would I have just declared it to be "weird" and moved on? Would I have dismissed it as a hyperactive subconscious? Jacob's response was unique. He woke up, then set up and anointed a memorial pillar. After that, he gave the place a name based on his encounter with the Lord. He called it Bethel, "the very gateway to heaven."

Nothing else mattered to Jacob at that moment. He was completely absorbed by the encounter where he had met God. He listened to everything God said. He didn't dismiss any of the promises and proceeded to live from a position of "Bethel," the place where he had a *gateway* to God. I believe Jacob effectively walked with God in Eden that night. It may have played out in a dream, but the dream was as real as the promises, which were as real as God, who is as real as His love for us.

NATHANAEL

In John 1:43-51, hundreds of years later, Jesus gave us the sequel to this story through another Eden moment. Often the sequels of our movies rarely exceed the quality of the original. But this sequel shows us that the staircase to Heaven wasn't just for Jacob. In John 1, Jesus is on the hunt for His twelve disciples. He's already gathered Andrew, Peter, James, John and Philip. Philip though, wants to find Nathanael and let him know that they found the Messiah. (I think it's funny they think they *found* Jesus!) Nathanael had a hard time believing that the Messiah could have come from Nazareth, of all places. He didn't believe that anything good could possibly come out of Nazareth.

So there was Nathanael, unbelieving and cynical of the story he had just heard. Jesus entered the scene but didn't use Nathanael's name to get his attention like He did with others. Rather, He used Nathanael's

God-given name, "Now here is a genuine son of Israel—a man of complete integrity." Nathanael was overcome, as Jesus released a taste of Eden to him. Everything else stopped as Nathanael's heart caught up with the encounter he was having! Then like with Jacob, Jesus gave him a promise, "I tell you the truth, you will all see heaven open and the angels of God going up and down on the Son of Man, the one who is the stairway between heaven and earth." This meant that the access to Heaven was real. The angels going up and down the staircase was real. But the difference was that the staircase, Heaven's access, has a name, Jesus. Jesus is the way that we have access to Heaven. We can walk again in the presence of God, just like Adam and Eve did, just like Jacob did, and just like He invited Nathanial to do. Nothing separating us from His love (Rom 8:35).

We know this verse and quote it often. But it is in verses like these and through people like Nathaniel we can see that access to God is available and unrestricted. There are no angels guarding the staircase to prevent us from gaining access to the holy places any longer. We have it already. We can walk again in Eden!

LEGION

In Mark 5:1-20, it's important to note that the man whom Jesus met in the Gerasene's was known as Legion, but that wasn't his name. He was known by this name because of the many demons that possessed him. There's one part of this story that has always intrigued me. Why did the man, supposedly under the control of demons, run toward Jesus rather than away from Him? If the demonic world is so strong, then how did this man escape with a thousand demons controlling him? The gospel accounts tell us that no one was strong enough to subdue him. But, physical force was not a necessity in any part of this man's deliverance. It was who Jesus was that brought this man to his

Eden moment. Here we are given a working understanding of the power of the Saviour's love. We get to see what the love of Jesus could do and overcome.

I think that the whole event would have messed with the disciples' understanding of religious law and self-preservation. To them, Jesus had crossed a lake to visit a cemetery, only to be confronted by a demon. I wonder how much of this day made sense to the disciples. I wonder if when they saw the man running they wanted to pick Jesus up and put Him back in the boat and row for their lives. I wonder if they would have put themselves in front of Jesus to protect Him. Then I wonder if they were confused by the confidence and authority Jesus walked in. They were watching a moment unfold that would have reinforced so much of what Jesus had taught. They were watching a moment of love that would change the course of many lives.

I have done deliverance ministry for many years. I have helped so many people find freedom from the demonic. I have seen first-hand the peaceful power of Jesus at work; doing what no other force on earth could come close to doing. But the question remained, "Why did Legion run to Jesus?" As I processed this question, slowly the answer dawned on me. The will that God had given to this man was stronger than the will or power of the demonic forces within the man. I realise now, that although I'd seen this many times, I'd only just understood it in the scripture. The possessed man carried a greater authority than the demons that possessed him. They couldn't stop the man from coming to Jesus. The best that the demons could do was make noise. The man's desire for freedom surpassed whatever desire or authority that the demons had to stop him from this meeting, and it seems that this man wasn't even a believer yet. Take a moment to understand the power and authority that your free will gives you. Then take a moment to discover what this free will can do for you in discovering Jesus. There is no demonic force that can overcome what Jesus has given to you. All hell couldn't stop this man from choosing to run out of a cemetery to Jesus, and run he did!

The demons tried to overwhelm the conversation so that Jesus would be conversing with them and not with the man. But Jesus did not converse with the demons, He commanded them. The demons asked for an outcome that didn't include hell. They knew that whatever happened next was at Jesus' bidding and not theirs. They asked to be sent into a herd of pigs and Jesus gave them what they asked for. To Jew, He was sending the demons into something unclean and would never be touched by Jew. Once there they were trapped and they couldn't leave the pigs that held them. From there the story shifted and the pigs went running off a cliff into the sea. This might sound odd to us today, but in the first century, the sea represented the abode of the dead. If you got lost in there, there was no coming back from that. Jesus gave them a working example of what an Eden moment looked like when the authority of Jesus was displayed and the result was a man clothed with a sane mind sitting at the feet of Jesus.

His family had abandoned him. His community had ostracised him. The law had attempted to enslave him. But the power of the love of Jesus brought a new encounter to this man. This was the only reason that Jesus came to this side of the lake. He came to one who was abandoned, cast out, homeless, and out of control. He came to set this captive free.

When Jesus went to get back in the boat, the man begged Jesus to take him with Him. To which Jesus gave a beautiful invitation, "No, go home to your family, and tell them everything the Lord has done for you and how merciful He has been." What Jesus was saying was that this was the time to let others share in his Eden moment. He was asked to take the evidence of his changed life to those who would be the most sceptical; his family. Imagine opening the door to the one that you had given up on, only to find that somehow his life had transformed. His Eden moment with Jesus now meant going home, and it wasn't stopping there. Mark's gospel account shows him then moving through Decapolis, telling everyone he met. The feedback from the people he met wasn't cynicism or doubt, it was amazement. These are the moments we are made for; moments where we encounter the love of Jesus every day of our lives. And like with the family of the man formerly known as Legion, we get to share in each other's Eden moments.

Eden moments, like these, affect generations of people. You could even say that it is affecting our generation. It has been a model for me in deliverance ministry. I've watched the authority of Jesus set people free to live with a sane mind.

ZACCHAEUS

In Luke 19:1-10, the hated tax collector Zacchaeus sought just a glimpse of Jesus. His day ended far differently than it had begun. He had lived and worked in Jericho; not a place known for much, except destruction. Nothing was going to stop him from seeing Jesus that day; not even being too short to see over the crowd. He climbed a sycamore tree in the hope of seeing Jesus. What happened next changed his life forever.

Jesus stopped, looked up, and asked him if He could come to his house for dinner. I'm fairly certain that wasn't what Zacchaeus expected. Everyone else despised Zacchaeus. If he had expected anything from Jesus, I think it would have been condemnation. Tax collectors weren't known for their culinary abilities, they were known as thieves. However, Jesus' paradigm and character was love, and the encounter He offered was love.

It's not recorded in the Bible what happened at that meal table, but we know what happened outside of the meal table. Religious leaders complained bitterly about this act of love. In the first century, to invite someone to your table gave them great honour and status. So what was Jesus doing at the same table as this tax collector? To the religious leaders, Jesus lowered Himself to the level of a tax collector. Or did He invite the tax collectors to be His family? Either way, it baffled them. Often when religious leaders were baffled, they chose condemnation over wisdom; which was always the wrong choice.

At that table was where revelation and love were given. I know this from the fruit that came from the table. At the end of the meal, Zacchaeus, while surrounded by many tax collector witnesses, decided to live from a place of restoration and generosity. He promised to repay all that he had stolen four times over and give half his wealth to the poor. So much love happened at the feast table and in Zacchaeus' life because Jesus' love was irresistible. He had a meal with the Son of God, where nothing separated him from God's love, an Eden moment for Zacchaeus that was not based on what he'd done, but based on how loved he was.

THE CHILDREN

In Luke 18:15-17, parents were bringing their children to be blessed by Jesus. This resulted in such an interesting response. The disciples were trying to be protective of Jesus and tried to send the parents and children away. This showed them caring for Jesus, but He was more interested in what this one moment could bring to the families who had come. Remember, Jesus was there to restore the connection between people and God. This was a moment to metaphorically walk in the cool of the evening with families. What made this such a brilliant Eden moment was that in such a small space of time, Jesus demonstrated that a simple act of love could become a generational blessing.

The parents knew that Jesus was special; I doubt that they would have brought their children to Him if they didn't. Like so many people before them, they knew that Jesus carried something that would add to their children's lives and they were willing to put up with the disciple's resentment to receive it. The Bible speaks of Jesus putting His hands on the children's heads and giving them a blessing, but we do not know what the blessing was. Maybe that's the point. Maybe the point of the story was more about Jesus' love than what Jesus said to bless them. The blessing that Jesus gave, was in effect, a generational one, as the parents received the blessing that Jesus gave to their children. The same love that welcomed the children welcomed the parents. And again, another Eden moment opened up for families of people, where they discovered that nothing could separate them from God's love.

THE ROMAN OFFICER

Luke 7:1-10 tells of a Roman officer who came to Jesus looking for the healing of a servant. Once again, you have a person coming to Jesus because they see something in Him that no one else seemingly carries. The brilliant part of this story is that the Roman officer could see Jesus carried authority.

The story was unusual in the fact that a Roman officer was coming to a Jew for help. Some 2000 years later, we can only really imagine whether this was odd or not. But what was to follow would amaze even Jesus! The Roman Centurion had a sick servant whom he valued enough to seek out healing from a healer who was becoming known as a troublemaker. As the story goes, Jesus agreed to come to the Centurion's home to heal the servant, but the narrative was interrupted when the Centurion told Jesus that He didn't need to touch the servant for healing to happen. You can hear this man's heart and faith being open to Jesus. The Centurion knew authority when he saw it. He also knew the power of a command issued from the mouth of one who walked in authority.

In this story, we have an extraordinary moment when Jesus was amazed at the faith He was witnessing! As we know from Hebrews 11, it is faith that pleases God. So in Jesus' amazement, there was so much of God's pleasure. Jesus tells everyone listening, "I tell you the truth, I haven't seen faith like this in all Israel!" This is no small statement to those listening. The Romans were "God-fearers" at best, but, this Roman was speaking the language of the Kingdom of God! Could this have been an Eden moment for Jesus?

Jesus went on to speak about the Kingdom's feast table, which Abraham, Isaac, and Jacob all sit at. This Roman soldier was sitting with these legends of the faith, and he was welcome there! And although the officer got his request of healing for his servant, he also received an affirmation from Jesus, that the Kingdom was his and that nothing separated him from it.

THE IMMORAL WOMAN

In Luke 7:36-50, Jesus was invited into the home of a Pharisee by the name of Simon. While the meal was underway, a woman, who the Bible calls immoral, entered the room. She knelt at Jesus feet, and broke open an expensive jar of perfume. Then with the perfume, and her tears, she anointed Jesus' feet. An extraordinary Eden moment for the woman and Jesus to share. The Pharisees condemned the woman for her lifestyle and they condemned Jesus — "a prophet should have known who was touching him." But, even a room full of condemnation couldn't steal the encounter that was unfolding. Her act of love and devotion to Jesus was met with the love and restoration that flowed naturally from Him. He spoke about the great love that flowed from her. He spoke of her faith which had cleansed her. When she left Simon's home, she knew she had encountered the love of God. Nothing else mattered at that moment. Not one shred of condemnation could get between the love that drew her to Jesus. She walked away having encountered the love that God had created Eden with. There was no fear between Jesus and this woman, as perfect love had driven away any kind of fear.

Our lives are full of these kinds of moments. Often, we don't even see them, or take the time to understand what God is doing through these encounters of love. These powerful moments that stand in the face of a world that empowers lives of fear. We become controlled by what we fear, rather than how we love. By listening to fear, our lives shrink as our friendships disappear. As Christians listening to fear we begin to learn a language that God doesn't speak. Again, the language of the culture that we spend the most time living in will be the language that we speak most fluently.

GIDEON

In Judges 6 & 7, we come across a man by the name of Gideon, whom we find hiding in a wine press where he was threshing wheat. It was in that wine press that an angel of the Lord found him. The angel says to Gideon, "Mighty hero, the Lord is with you." To which Gideon replies, "Sir, if the Lord is with us, why has all this happened to us? Where are the miracles our ancestors told us about? Didn't they say, 'the Lord brought us up out of Egypt'? But now the Lord has abandoned us and handed us over to Midianites."

Inside this one little paragraph, you can hear the language of Gideon's unbelief. He doesn't seem to hear the angel call him a "mighty hero." What he is concentrating on is the phrase "the Lord is with you." From the evidence of his life, he could not believe the words he was hearing. It seems the evidence of God's presence wasn't a reality for Gideon or his people. It's in Gideon's words and language that we are given an understanding of what he believes. He's heard the stories of his people in the past and seemed happy to believe that they happened. But for him, deliverance, miracles, and protection were stories from the past. His language sounded more like unbelief, disappointment, or fear. These are not languages that God speaks.

The angel turned to him and said, "Go with the strength you have and rescue Israel from the Midianites. I am sending you." Yet again, Gideon listened and then responded with unbelief and fear when he asked the Lord how *he* could rescue Israel: "My clan is the weakest in the whole tribe of Manasseh, and I'm the least in my entire family!" Once again, God didn't talk to his unbelief or fear, He spoke to who he was and the relationship that He was offering. Gideon's Eden moment is starting to come into view.

As the story goes on, Gideon tested God by asking Him to remain where He was while he went and prepared a meal. Now, this was no small meal and it would have taken hours to prepare. Gideon cooked a goat and then baked a loaf of bread. I wonder if Gideon is like us. Sometimes we know what God wants us to do, but if we put enough time between the hearing and the doing, then maybe God will ask someone else. In this story, we have no idea what was going through

Gideon's mind, but when we read all of his story, we can see that fear was a theme throughout it. We could safely say that ever since the angel of the Lord turned up at the wine press, it was likely that Gideon was in fear.

Gideon came back and found the angel right where he left him. He placed the goat and the bread on a stone. To which the angel touches it with his staff and the meal goes up in smoke and fire. At this point, Gideon has an "eyes wide open" moment and the revelation hits him that it is truly God in front of him. This is the moment of Eden for Gideon, where nothing was separating him from God. He was in conversation with God. It didn't seem to bother God what he was doing, or even the language of fear that flowed from Gideon. We see Romans 8:38 happen thousands of years before Paul wrote the letter... nothing separated Gideon from God's love. Unbelief and fear didn't separate Gideon from Him. It affected the relationship, but it did not change the way God interacted with him or loved him.

Gideon's theology, though, wasn't tracking with his experience. You see, he believed that to see God was to die and this theology brought him to the bone-crunching revelation, "Oh, Sovereign Lord, I'm doomed! I have seen the angel of the Lord face to face!" (Judg 6:22). His theology was built on the belief that there was only one outcome for someone sitting in front of God—death. Even though Abraham, Moses, and Joshua had all done it and had lived. But to Gideon, he was the least of the least. His language had convinced him that this was his truth. However, God was speaking a new word to him, one that he had probably not heard before: "mighty hero." Gideon's language and belief system needed to change and reflect the truth which God spoke over Him. The only outcome that Gideon's brain could land on was that he was about to lose his life.

If death is the outcome of a revelation from God, then I'd be wondering about the Kingdom that we're called to participate in. God hadn't revealed Himself to Gideon only to kill him for grasping the revelation. He revealed Himself to Gideon so that his belief system and language would begin to mirror the conversation that they were having. Gideon was deep in his Eden moment, and his theology was rapidly changing as he was engaging in the experience.

This is what I've seen time and time again in my journey. Each encounter with God seems to challenge the very essence of what I believe and then how I behave in that realignment of my beliefs. Romans 12:2 says, "Don't copy the behaviour and customs of this world, but let God transform you into a new person by changing the way you think. Then you will learn to know God's will for you, which is good and pleasing and perfect." This is what is happening to Gideon and to each of us when we encounter God in these ways, He is changing the way that we think. Gideon is being challenged out of a belief system that said God used to do these things and He used people way more important than Gideon. It challenged him to think of his relationship with God and how present God was with him.

God reassured Gideon that he had nothing to fear. This is a revelation that seems to follow most revelations of God. Now, this is an interesting word to give when it seemed that Gideon had everything to fear. His nation had been overrun by an occupying force, and he was threshing wheat in the bottom of a wine press for fear of being discovered by the enemy. This alone seemed to indicate the very real presence of the enemy in the land. He was simply trying to feed his family. So the fear of not being able to do so drove him to be doing something that could get him into trouble.

What happens when God drops a word like that on us? Here's my take on "do not be afraid." This is God's way of saying to us, "Do not let fear change the course of direction of your life." For Gideon to now live from this new paradigm of relationship with God, fear needed to be challenged first. So Gideon started by building an altar right in that place and called it *Yahweh-Shalom*, which means "God is peace." I believe that when Gideon declared "God is peace," he was testifying and not prophesying.

For when God spoke the words, "Do not be afraid," I believe the atmosphere was affected by the words of the Creator. When God speaks, creation happens. The atmosphere changed so much that Gideon built an altar that would remind him, and anyone else, that in this place he met and spoke with God, and peace is what resulted. Gideon did not want to forget his Eden moment.

Gideon's story then gets bigger. He was told that he's a "mighty hero" and that victory over the Midianites would be won through him. What he wasn't told was how this victory would happen. Have you ever wanted all of the plans before you took one step towards the goal? Maybe you could understand then and relate to what Gideon was going through.

To start with, God told him later that evening that he had to burn down his father's Asherah pole and kill one of his bulls! So basically, Gideon was about to mess with his dad's belief system. Asherah was a Canaanite goddess that supposedly created other gods and the pole represented the Tree of Life. The combination of both is a poor representation of Israel's allegiance to God, who created the Tree of Life. Gideon was not only messing with the family's belief system but also the family's income by killing the bull and burning it as a sacrifice. It didn't appear that Gideon's day was getting any simpler. But, God kept speaking and Gideon kept listening. His Eden moment was growing, and he was learning to listen to God's voice.

Fear's voice, the talking snake, would have tried to make him doubt God's voice. I'm sure that Gideon was wrestling with upsetting his dad and his family. But as we read the story, Gideon now knew the voice and the presence of God, and he was willing to trust it. The Asherah pole came down and the bull was sacrificed. When the morning came, people started looking for the culprit and demanded that death should come to the one who did the deed. Gideon's life continued to be complicated, but his relationship with God was becoming clearer. God had told him that He hadn't given him the revelation to kill him. So Gideon fronted up to his dad, only to find that his dad was sick and tired of the very god that Gideon had pulled down! Gideon's dad had more faith in his son than he had in the god of his Asherah pole. Now he was inviting his community to believe in the words that God had spoken over Gideon.

Not long after this, the Midianites allied with the Amalekites and decided that it was time to attack Israel again. It's hard to imagine the anxiety that the Israelites would have felt in watching the approaching armies. They were not strong; they were the ones hiding from these people. You can see that Gideon's life had gained momentum, with one step leading to the next step. Each step was taken in faith that it was God ordering the events in front of him. It all started when he was hiding in a wine press threshing wheat. Gideon was once again listening to the language of his heart. Did he still believe in the words that God spoke over him, back there in the wine press?

So here's the next Eden moment. Judges 6:34 says, "Then the Spirit of the Lord clothed Gideon with power." What an interesting verse. I'm pretty certain that this wasn't Gideon getting around in a new wardrobe. I think it was Gideon now living out his identity. He'd discovered that God was a God of peace, now he was about to see that He was also a God of power.

Gideon blew a ram's horn and gathered his people for battle. Things were getting more and more real for Gideon. From threshing wheat at the bottom of a wine press to the leader of Israel's army. That evening though, the old language of fear and unbelief resurfaced. He went back to his home and asked God for confirmation. In days past, it was easier to let these armies just come and take whatever they wanted. But God didn't reveal Himself to Gideon to show him the path of least resistance, He revealed Himself to Gideon because He knew He had a person who would believe Him and carry this revelation well. Two nights running, a conversation happened in which Gideon asked God to prove the word that He gave him, and it seemed, God happily participated. Gideon's Eden moments were becoming normal and they weren't finished yet.

The most well-known story of Gideon then unfolds. Thirty-two thousand Israelite men turn up for the battle. However, the people of Israel were speaking the same language that Gideon met God with; they were afraid. Gideon's Eden moments had kept occurring, but this conversation in the community would do nothing to help Gideon's anxiety. God told him that there were too many Israelites. His army was too large! He told Gideon to send home those who were afraid, and twenty-two thousand went home. Ten thousand remained. God again tells him that he's got too many men. By the end of the day, of the thirty-two thousand that started with him, only three hundred remained! Yet God still promised him victory, and Gideon kept putting one foot in front of the other and walked with God in his Eden moment.

Later that evening his next Eden moment happened. God came to him and recognised straight away that Gideon's old enemy and language of fear was once again being spoken. So, what did God do? He led him to the place of revelation, by encouraging him to sneak into the enemies' camp and listen to the enemy's language. He got there and saw an enemy so large that it was described as a "swarm of locusts." Their camels were "like grains of sand on the seashore—too many to count." If Gideon was prone to anxiety, then this view would not have been helpful. But God did not lead him there to die and He didn't lead him there to use his eyes; He led him there to listen. Gideon crept down and listened to the soldiers of the enemy talk. The language he would have expected was that of an easy victory the next day, but that wasn't the language he heard. What he heard was the same language that he used to speak, the language of fear and unbelief. The soldiers were having dreams and each of the dreams was prophesying defeat, not victory. As one dream became many dreams, the enemy was being defeated by their own belief system.

Gideon's battle plan then came into view. They didn't need to fight, they needed to trust. Three hundred people with a ram's horn and a clay pot. This would become a story of legend, but it was hardly a battle plan that many would have had faith in. By this stage though, Gideon's Eden moments had come full circle. The "mighty hero" was standing as a hero long before the first horn was blown. He knew who he was, and he knew that God had not led him to this place to die. He knew that victory was in sight. At midnight, Gideon, clothed with

110

power, blew the first ram's horn. Which was met with two hundred and ninety-nine others. They then smashed the clay jars, and everything in the enemies camp turned in on itself. Quite simply, confusion destroyed what fear had manifested in the enemy camp.

By the end of the next day, the people were declaring that Gideon was the "mighty hero" whom God had declared him to be. This is such a powerful revelation of our design and how God sees us. Gideon was created as a mighty hero; it was his design. God didn't tell him that he would be a mighty hero in the future, He said that He was already. God was not talking to his potential, He was speaking to his design and calling that design forward. Years of oppression and fear had messed with his divine design. Now God was realigning his identity and giving him a revelation that would end in abundant life.

Gideon had one Eden moment after another. In each one, God was fully present and relational. Nothing separated Gideon from God's love. By the end of this story, Gideon knew God as peace, power, and promise.

EDEN MANIFESTED

Before Gideon was seen to be the mighty hero to a nation, he was seen to be a mighty hero to his family. He might not have seen it that way, but any parent knows the ache of the heart that surrounds providing for their family. To have a roof over their heads and food on the table is one of the most basic human needs, and there was Gideon, faithfully providing for his family. Threshing wheat on the wine press floor was where God found him and where Gideon encountered Him. This was a long way away from Moses encountering God on Mount Sinai. But again, Mount Sinai was a long way away from Moses encountering God at the burning bush. The *mighty hero* was seen by God long before anyone else had a glimpse of what he could look like. These powerful moments are an overflow of what happens in relationship with God when no one else is watching.

Eden moments surround us all and are waiting to be experienced. They are not just for the heroes of the faith from the Bible. To believe you can't encounter God like Gideon was able to is to believe a lie. Often this belief is hidden in our theologies or our disappointments with God. Gideon had both, yet still, he was open to participating with what God had for him. Don't let the encounters of the Bible be the only encounters that you believe in. God wants to encounter you, probably even more than you want to encounter Him! He went to the length of giving up His own Son, which is no small gift.

When I was younger I didn't believe for these things. The Bible stories were so spectacular and my life seemed to be so boring in comparison. I always wanted to experience the spectacular but just didn't believe that it was for me. Unbelief has this very powerful way of keeping us from living out full lives. It has a way of convincing you that others believe better than you do. It always had me on the outside looking in to see what Jesus was doing rather than being in there with Him. I marvelled at the faith of the four friends in Mark 2 who refused to stand on the outside and look in. They were the ones who dug a hole through the roof of someone's house so that their friend could be healed by Jesus.

My belief system needed to change and it needed to be challenged. I now believe that every challenge that comes into my life is an opportunity for me to grow. I think it's why James was able to say that these were moments of "pure joy" (Jas 1:2), simply because he saw the transformation that occurred through challenge. Let me share with you some of the Eden moments that I have had, which could initially be explained as challenges, but ended up being pure joy.

As I shared earlier, my wife, Trish, and I are 13 years on the right side of a marriage crisis. All those years ago, we had a crash course on learning to love each other in a new way. We learned to enjoy spending time with each other. To do this, we had to work on getting to know each other better than before. Marriage crisis is not what I would call "pure joy" in any conversation. However, once I went through my own breakdown with it, I started to see God at work.

Initially, it was a tough pill to swallow. I had numerous people praying for me and they were sending visions of what they saw Jesus doing for me. In those early days, each of those visions were hard to hear as they were revealing my pain and dysfunction. It got to the point where a dear friend rang me and said that they saw me with my hands over my ears. I didn't want to hear any more of the disaster that my life was and so, in the vision, I had stopped listening for Jesus. However the vision went further and spoke of a wooden sword that Jesus was attempting to give me, but because I wasn't listening I wasn't receiving. This one moment in time is one of my most powerful Eden moments. A wooden sword means that I would no longer have to fight, as God would be fighting for me. Shortly after this I met Steve, whom I spoke of in an earlier chapter. I met him in a professional capacity and I am still with him as a close friend. He was my wooden sword; he was the one that God raised up to walk with me. Through him, Eden moments started to become a whole lot more real for me.

In 2014 our marriage was beginning to heal, and Trish and I decided that we needed to start exploring and being adventurous. It was time to make some new memories. New Zealand was a place we always wanted to go and now was the time to step out and embrace it. To date, we've been back numerous times and we are always planning our next trip. Not only is it outstandingly beautiful, it is the place where we have encountered Eden moments regularly.

The "pure joy" that we receive now when we holiday is not pure-ly based on location and activity, but on our relationship. It's not something that we could even see prior to 2008. Back then we were just trying to survive. But it's in the hidden moments on wine press floors, when no one else is watching, that you become ready for God to release more in you. Back then, my future looked questionable. I thought I would have to change careers and start all over again. In so many ways, hopelessness and discouragement tried to steal the voice of hope from within me. But God kept on showing up. He kept on inviting me to walk with Him as Adam and Eve had done so all those years ago.

In 2016, Trish and I travelled to England to spend some time with our daughter, who was living there at the time. We hired a car and drove up to Scotland and back. It was an amazing time! But there were two moments for me when I knew that I had encountered God. The first happened on the Scottish Borders. We were driving the scenic route from Edinburgh to York when we came across the town of Jedburgh. When you drive into the town, you can't help but see a magnificent, albeit ruined, abbey. So I hit the indicator (turn signal) and, much to our children's groaning disappointment, we stopped to take a look. It was a cold January. There was ice and snow on the ground. The kids headed off to find a coffee shop, and Trish and I went to explore.

Standing in the middle of this ruined abbey, I started to use my imagi-nation. Coming from a building and engineering background, I imag-ined what this place would have been like in its heyday. I imagined monks going about their everyday lives and people coming into the church, listening to sermons and praying. It was there, standing in the cold, that I asked God to speak to me. It's one of the things that I love to do in ancient places of worship when thinking about the hundreds, if not thousands, of years that people had interacted with the site. All around me, and under me, were the graves of those who had faithfully worshipped here.

So I closed my eyes and listened. As soon as I did, I heard a crow cry out its mournful song. It's not the voice I wanted to hear, as crows often speak of death. So I told God that this wasn't the word I wanted to hear and closed my eyes again to listen. Again... it was the crow. So instead of telling God again that I didn't want to hear that from Him, I looked to find where the crow was. It was sitting and singing on top of a stone cross that was on the gable at the far end of the ruined abbey. So I waited and asked God to speak to me of the crow and the cross.

As I opened my eyes, I saw the crow fly from the cross and a voice came into my mind saying, "I used to be worshipped here, but now I am only remembered here." It is a phrase I will never forget. But God didn't stop there. He then said, "Will I be worshipped by the things that you are doing, or will I merely be remembered?" The crow leaving the cross became a profound word for me. I knew that death could no longer sit on what Jesus had done to restore life. As Jesus' follower, I was to bring life and scatter the birds that brought fear and death. Right there on that cold winter morning, I had encountered God! It was an Eden moment for me.

A day later, Trish and I were sitting in York Minster, enjoying our very first Evensong. We settled in for a new experience. York Minster is a magnificent building! The stained glass windows are amazing. But again, coming from my background, I was wondering how on earth they built this a thousand years ago! The stonework is extraordinary! The choir was singing a song that had been penned five hundred years ago from one of the psalms. It was a beautiful experience. We were there sitting in the Chancel of York Minster doing what people had done for hundreds of years. Again, I asked God for a word and straight away a voice came into my mind, "Kings and queens have sat where you are sitting and now you have permission to do the same." Like the day before, the words He spoke were ones I have remembered. It was another Eden moment for me. When I put both of those Eden moments together I can have a greater understanding of what He was showing me: "You have the permission and authority of the Kingdom to lead people to meet me."

In 2019, Trish and I were in Rome. We were, of course, visiting ancient churches. Some of them were reclaimed from Roman gods and other belief systems. They had been there for hundreds or thousands of years. In Rome, I walked into one and was astounded by its size, the art displayed, and the gold ceiling! Again, I marvelled at how they could have built it. It was over 1500 years old! This church had its museum of holy relics, with some of the items kept for their healing power. We spent quite some time walking through the church. When it was the time that I would usually ask God for a word, I found myself feeling nauseous. It could have been jetlag or eating a lot of food at vastly different times of the day. However, in that nauseous moment, I asked God for a word anyway. Again, straight into my mind came the phrase, "Why are you looking for someone alive in the place of the dead. This is not a church, it is a museum." Once again His words were profound and from that point on in our holiday, I stopped going into places of worship and merely enjoyed them for the history that they so amazingly displayed.

I've had many more encounters with God. These three are a way of showing you that God loves to speak and He usually speaks to me in themes. Three different encounters in places where people have long worshipped, and the conversation with God got a whole lot bigger for me. Not only was I told that I had authority in His Kingdom and that I would lead people to Him, I now knew that I would be leading people from religion into a relationship with Him.

Please hear that I'm not hating on the church. I believe in The Church, His Bride. What I no longer believe is that religion carries the answers to getting us back to Eden. I believe God is doing a new work that emphasises our experiences in relationship with Him. I believe that the works of Jesus, all those years ago, is the reforming, recentering, and pioneering action that is leading back into Eden.

Listen to what Jesus told the Samaritan woman in John 4: "Jesus replied, 'Believe me, a time is coming when you will worship the Father neither on this mountain nor in Jerusalem. You Samaritans worship what you do not know; we worship what we do know, for salvation is from the Jews. Yet a time is coming and has now come when the true worshipers will worship the Father in the Spirit and truth, for they are the kind of worshipers the Father seeks. God is spirit, and his worshipers must worship in the Spirit and truth." (John 4:21-24) Here in this extraordinary moment of encounter, Jesus also revealed to her that He was indeed the Messiah (John 4:26) that everyone was looking for! This didn't happen in a synagogue or a church, but it did happen in spirit and truth.

For so long I believed that God was found at church. Little did I realise that He could be found anywhere I am. He wants to be found by us. He wants to be encountered by us. He wants us to know the love we were designed for can be found wherever we are.

God is love (1 John 4:16), and if He is, then the Son is also love. Jesus said, "I tell you the truth, the Son can do nothing by himself. He does only what he sees the Father doing. Whatever the Father does, the Son also does." (John 5:19). He also said, "Anyone who has seen me has seen the Father!" (John 14:9). The Father and Son are the same; they are love. As Jesus is love, everything that Jesus did and said should be interpreted through this lens.

To a Samaritan woman, He was able to reveal her whole life story and yet she didn't feel shame. Just let that settle on your spirit for a moment. At what point, when someone's dirty laundry is spoken out does shame not have a voice? It's unheard of for many of us, but *for the one who was love personified His voice carried no condemnation.*

Paul once said, "...there is now no condemnation for those who are in Christ Jesus" (Rom 8:1 NIV). Now, he has also called himself "the worst" of all sinners (1 Tim 1:15). How is it that a person can be the worst of all sinners and yet they still conclude that there was no condemnation in his story? The answer is simple and yet profound: he encountered Jesus, love personified. Paul had his Eden moment on the road to Damascus and walked from that moment in freedom and love, never returning to the life that he left behind.

Let's go a little deeper with this thinking. There are many things that Jesus did that could be easily interpreted as love. When He raised a widow's son back to life (Luke 7:11-17), it can easily be understood as a loving thing to do. The same when He fed the five thousand (Mark 6:30-44); it was another powerful outworking of His love. In both examples, there was a need that He could do something about and let love flow out of Him.

But what about the difficult meetings that Jesus had, the ones we have traditionally translated as a judgment or even condemnation? For example, when we read that He confronted the Pharisees and called them "whitewashed tombs" (Matt 23:27), was He loving them? What would this story read like if we understood the love that Jesus had for the leaders that were in front of Him? When I read it through a lens of love, I hear Jesus' heart breaking for those He loves. I hear Him crying out for them to come out from behind their façade and live out of the freedom and love that He offered. I must believe that He loved them. This means that I must believe the way He spoke to them was in their best interests. He wanted to see them restored in relationship with God, not cast away from Him. He didn't come to earth to condemn them, but He came to save them (John 3:17).

Before you dismiss this thought bubble and go straight back to putting the Pharisees in the place we have traditionally kept them, look at it in the context of our day. At times, we find it very easy to point out faults and judge our leaders. They may have made poor choices, yet they still desire to see His Kingdom come. Dig for long enough in any life and you will find plenty of reasons to judge the person you were designed to love. Leaders are just easy marks for us to find fault in. With Jesus, I believe He was purely loving them out of their religious thinking and into a new way of relationship.

Remember, every act of love is an act of God. Rereading Jesus' interaction with the Pharisees through this lens had me undone, and I knew that Jesus' heart must have broken at that moment. Even when He died, one of His final phrases was, "Father, forgive them, for they don't know what they are doing" (Luke 23:34). This wasn't anger, nor was it just quoting from scripture to fulfill an ancient prophecy. This

121

was the heart of a man who loved so supremely that He forgave completely. This is the One that we follow and this is the likeness we are being transformed into. As Jesus is love, so are we.

This is loving at a whole new level, and for Trish and me, it became the only place we wanted to live from. We don't need to defend our hearts from each other at every moment, now we can open our hearts to each other. We don't always do this perfectly, but it has now become the lens we use to discover the intimacy that God planned for us. This is Eden. From the place of hope, we discovered this was not a fairy tale, it was the truth.

This revelation brought much happiness, but our relationship is not dependent on happiness. It's dependent on the love we share with God and each other. From the orientation of love, we have discovered that regardless of our circumstances, we can find the strength and the joy of our relationship. When we allow our circumstances to control the way we engage in a relationship, we start listening to what we don't have, rather than what we do have. To me, this was the one very real conversation that Eve entertained with the devil. When you start valuing your circumstances more than your relationship, then the relationship will suffer.

Many times, I have heard a couple say, "If we have a baby, we'll make this marriage work," as if the addition of another human to the already conflicted relationship will magically align them behind the greater good of the child. My response to this is always, "If you make this relationship strong, then the marriage will work. Then, and only then, should you talk about adding other humans to this relationship." If you cannot do a relationship with one other person, then adding another would only make it more complicated.

122

So often we look to add something to our lives to make us feel better: a new car, new house, new guitar, new holiday, new job, new watch, new whatever! But each of them does not supply what we are searching for... we are looking for what only God gives. Love is the bond that binds us together. This was and has always been our design. God is love, He created us with love, and all things exist through love. Our circumstances should be a distant second to love.

I believe Paul showed us this revelation when he said, "I have learned how to be content with whatever I have" (Phil 4:11). He wrote this from jail when his circumstances were giving him nothing to feel content about. Trish and I stood in that jail cell, and I can tell you it in no way would have been an enjoyable or comfortable experience. But Paul discovered something in God's relationship with him there that he could testify to. Could it be that in Paul's jail cell he found Eden? In this phrase of Paul, he is also prophesying that as Jesus has done for him, so can He do for us. Your circumstances should never come between your relationship with God.

The next revelation that came to me through understanding this was that each of us carries the authority and power to create these safe places of relationship for others. Jesus said, "Your love for one another will prove to the world that you are my disciples" (John 13:35). Here Jesus is speaking of a love that can be seen, testified to, and reproduced! I also believe that when God told us to "be fruitful and multiply" (Gen 1:28), He wasn't just talking about having children. He was speaking to every area of our lives: multiply relationships, multiply forgiveness, multiply grace and kindness. We have all we need to make this happen.

Quite simply, love creates and God has put His creative power in each of us. Adam and Eve were created to create. Humanity would come from their union, but for hope and faith to be manifest, it would need the creative power of love. For families to grow, for houses to become homes, this creative power would build and mould communities around a belief in a God who loves, protects, and empowers.

When nothing is holding us where we are, other than the relationship we have, then we have used love to create something eternal. We have walked through difficult times and sown this creative power into each moment to see fear flee from our relationship. We have multiplied forgiveness, grace, mercy, and kindness. In doing so, we will also notice that others are impacted by what we have created. Love is infectious; it is easily seen and people are quickly drawn to it. This happens because their nature has been drawn back to the source. God's love is the manifested power of His presence. Each of us long to be loved, and then in turn we long to love. It's our design, and it has always been His plan. It's difficult for us not to love.

For Trish and I, the discovery of this in our marriage has been the springboard to testify of it to other marriages. We describe it as Eden because we live from a place where guilt and shame are no longer welcome, but God is seen and heard. Like the Eden that Adam and Eve knew, it's not a place that is devoid of evil. Satan was allowed to be there, and he spoke to Eve in a way that had her second-guessing who she was and all she had access to. Adam and Eve should have invested more in what God had to say, and ignored what Satan had to say. They should have valued their relationship with God more than the words of one who was just planting seeds of doubt. Truths like these can and should be tested. The evidence of the supposed truths that Satan brought was doubt and envy. The evidence of the truths that God brought was peace and love. Intimacy flows from places where love thrives, and it dries up when fear and doubt are given a voice.

You have been given a freedom that you are free to do anything with. That's the whole concept of freedom, you are free to do whatever you like. In a relationship, this freedom can be used to create or control. In Eden, Adam and Eve were free to do anything they wanted and go wherever they wanted. If they wanted to, they could have gone far beyond the borders that surrounded Eden. But there was something about the manifest presence of God that kept drawing them into the place of encountering Him. It is the same invitation that we have been given. We can encounter Him every moment of our lives, as wherever we are, He is found.

KINGDOM HERE

Flowing on from understanding your design is to then understand the Kingdom you are designed to live from. This is something that Jesus tackled head-on when He was teaching and leading. There were many parables which started with the phrase "The Kingdom of God is like..." I love that there were so many! It shows that one metaphor was never going to be enough to effectively describe something indescribable. He described it as a "pearl of great value," a "treasure in a field," and a "mustard seed," just to list a few. Jesus used every possible story to help His audience understand that this wasn't some far-off, distant, metaphoric land. He was speaking to the people about the way the Kingdom looked and operated.

In Matthew 6:9-10, Jesus is asked by His disciples to teach them how to pray. To which, He gave them a prayer that generation after generation has learned to recite. Even if you aren't a Christian, the Lord's Prayer is fairly recognisable by most. To the disciples, though, it was a powerful lesson in conversing with God. These men were Jews and they would have grown up being taught how to pray in their religious expression. So why were they asking to learn a whole new way of praying? I think it's because Jesus was using a language that used the same words that they were familiar with, but they had a greater meaning than what they had known. The gospel writer recorded Jesus' words as a monologue, but that's not what Jesus was modelling when He told them He only does what He sees the Father doing and speaks what the Father is saying.

I believe the Lord's Prayer is a powerful introduction to understanding the way the Kingdom operates in the present day. In it, He calls us to understand the Kingdom. He taught the disciples to ask God for His Kingdom to come soon and for His will to be done on earth as it's been done in Heaven. For years I interpreted this as being when I died and went to Heaven, but now I understand that this is a prayer to return to Eden in the present.

Not long after this teaching, a man who was demonically possessed was brought to Jesus. Because of the demon, this man was blind and could not speak. What happened next can reveal which kingdom we are operating from. Always look for the fruit of someone's life to see what kingdom they're operating from. Jesus got rid of the demon and healed the man, so the fruit we can see is freedom, healing, and restoration. All of these are powerful traits of God that we see throughout the Bible. Planning someone's death was not a fruit of the Spirit or a character trait of God.

I find it intriguing when the Holy Spirit moves in undeniable power that people will either want to encounter it or drive it away. I've commonly found that what humans don't understand they will quickly reject. It seems that this is what Jesus encountered fairly regularly until the person who did the rejecting had a need that only God could address. When Jairus sought out Jesus, he did so as a father and not as a Pharisee. His chosen career of being a Pharisee and leader of the religion became secondary when he had a need that his religion could do nothing about.

It's amazing how quickly we will start accepting what the Spirit is doing when we are unable to fix the circumstances we are in. We also have someone like Nicodemus, who was much more open-minded and chose to come to Jesus with questions rather than needs. He seemed to be intrigued about the works and teachings Jesus was doing. He even attributed them to God. The way that Jesus engaged with both of these learned men shows us something of how the Kingdom works. Jesus met Jairus in his need and Nicodemus in his questions.

In the story of the demon-possessed man, once he was freed and healed, the crowd wanted to crown Jesus as the Messiah. Belief was soaring as they saw such a powerful confirmation and were witnesses to the work of God. However, the Pharisees, witnessing the same expression of healing, wanted to label Jesus a disciple of Satan. Again, if you've ever found yourself amid conflicting opinions like this, simply look for the fruit of the power. If the fruit of the power aligns with the character of Jesus, then run with it. If it doesn't, then drop it like a stone. You don't need to stand there and argue it, just test it and move with the fruit of what you saw Jesus doing.

Jesus then taught them how kingdoms rise and fall. He pointedly told them that Satan can't cast out Satan and that it made no sense. Why would Satan be interested in setting people free from the power that he had trapped them in? Not only was the man now in his right senses, but he was also seeing and speaking. So then, in weighing the evidence, Jesus said, "If I am casting out demons by the Spirit of God, then the Kingdom has arrived among you" (Matt 12:28).

Can you hear what Jesus just revealed to everyone listening? Some time between Matthew 6, when Jesus taught them to pray for the Kingdom to come, and Matthew 12, when He declared that the Kingdom had come, something had changed. Eternally Jesus was inviting them into the Kingdom that is, not the Kingdom that will be. His Kingdom was here and this Kingdom's King was standing right in front of them, and His Kingdom was now revealed by Him.

Jesus said that the Kingdom is here "among" us, such a powerful and intriguing statement. To the Jew, these were statements of freedom from Rome, establishing themselves as a world power again. To Jesus, though, it was an invitation to live in the Kingdom that would be known for the character traits of its King. He is a conquering King, that is true. But His conquering didn't happen in unseating governments through force. He conquered through the love and authority that He carried so powerfully.

He took the Kingdom from the hands of the religious leaders and placed it into the hands of fishermen and tax collectors. He put it into the hands of the unqualified and uneducated to show how accessible the Kingdom is. When He was asked about the greatest in the Kingdom, He didn't point to some ancient hero of the faith, He invited a child to sit with Him as a living example of the greatness of the Kingdom among them.

I believe that He is still doing this today. Like in Jesus' time, religious leaders today may not react well to this kind of dialogue. Their careers are dependent upon keeping the platforms they have created. But the Kingdom is not dependent upon any platform. The Kingdom thrives at dinner tables, in cafes, in meeting places, and in deep conversations. For Jesus to become known as a "glutton and a drunkard" (Matt 11:19), He must have enjoyed engaging with people in the place of the table. A place where nothing separated them from His love. A moment of Eden happened every time Jesus sat down for a meal. A moment where the Kingdom was expressed through the love of its King.

Paul tells me that nothing separates me from my King's love. The writer of Hebrews tells me that I can walk boldly into my King's throne room (Heb 3:19). Revelation 2:17 tells me that my King knows me by name. Peter tells me that I "share His divine nature" (2 Pet 1:4). John tells me that His love "expels all fear" (1 John 4:18) and then He says that if I still fear, that I have a "fear of punishment, and this shows that we have not fully experienced his perfect love." My conclusion is that I do not need to fear my King; He loves me, and I am freely able to encounter my King's love.

The Kingdom is here now surrounding us. It is everywhere we look and it is deep within us. We will recognise it by the love that we encounter with each other. We will hear it in the language used. Our access to the Kingdom is not based on what church we go to, or what theologies we hold to. It involves learning to love yourself and others the way Jesus has loved you. There's a very famous quote of Billy Graham that says, "It is the Holy Spirit's job to convict, God's job to judge, and my job to love." I love this quote and I use it often, especially when people are judging others by the lifestyles or choices that they have made.

I have sat with many people who identify as homosexual and listened to their hearts break over the rejection they have received at the hands of the church. I've so often thought about the Billy Graham quote. No one on the planet wants to be judged for their choices, but it seems a majority of the church has made this their responsibility, so often casting away what they don't understand. They choose to judge long before choosing to love. There have been times when I've heard the judging being referred to as supposedly loving them.

Take a moment to look at the fruit that flows when we decide to lift ourselves from the place of loving well to judging. Never does this fruit taste good. Condemnation leaves bitterness in our mouths. Judgment leaves people feeling helpless and hopeless. Then, shame confuses their true identity from who they are in Christ to who they are in our eyes. It all needs to stop. Unless it does, we will continue building the wrong kingdom. This judging kingdom is seen by its fruit of control and manipulation. It's cultish to change a person's will and behaviour by manipulating them to think and live in a certain way. The Kingdom that Jesus ushered in invited us to let go of control and just love the person who stands right in front of us. It is utterly different from what the world so often sees as the church. The kingdoms are worlds apart.

So, how about we stop only praying "Kingdom come" and start living in the "Kingdom here," which is known by His love, which flows through His people. The Kingdom isn't defined by a location, it is encountered by the presence of love. It is tangible and can be experienced every moment of every day.

For so many years I hoped for His Kingdom to come. Now I realise I was hoping for what I already had. His Kingdom is and has always been within me. I hadn't realised how accessible the Kingdom was! Even as a new pastor, all those years ago, fear controlled so many of my decisions. I feared the church shrinking. I feared the church running out of money. I feared that my vision wasn't big enough. I feared that my messages weren't good enough. It's not hard to see that the language that I was speaking was as far from the King as it could have been. I was fluent in the language of fear! I was leading an expression of His Kingdom, but every conversation I had about the church was laced with fear. Even when the church was going well, the same language continually chipped away at what the Spirit of God was doing.

So here's a revelation that I discovered the hard way: if fear is our language, then fear is found in our story, and it will always control the outcomes and plans of our lives. We weren't designed to let fear control us. We were designed to recognise fear for what it is. If it is real, we are designed to discern it and do what is needed to handle the cause of the fear. If it is false, we are designed to let love drive it away. When we are controlled by fear we will rarely be able to see or live in the fullness that Jesus came to lead us into.

Let's finish this chapter with an activation that I use most days of my own life. The writer of Hebrews tells us that we can walk boldly into the throne room of Heaven (Heb 4:16). I'd like to invite you to imagine what the throne room of Heaven looks like. Take the time to create the picture in your mind. Don't let your imagination be bound by anything with this. Maybe it looks like a ballroom, a feast table, or even a garden. Maybe it looks like an enormous throne with the elders and surrounding Jesus on the throne. There are no wrong answers to using your imagination in this. If you're comfortable, allow all of your senses to get involved. What does it feel, taste, sound, or smell like? If you can, imagine colours. Notice how things look utterly different when colour is introduced. Let all of your senses come alive in your imagination and engage with all that may be happening in the throne room.

Then I invite you to look for Jesus. Take notice of where He is and what He's doing. Again, if you feel comfortable, go to Him and engage with Him. He's always loving and always welcoming. You have nothing to fear in coming to Him. Then lastly, if you feel safe, ask Him to reach out and touch you, give you a gift, or speak a word to you. Notice where He touches and what it feels like. He's always appropriate, so you need not fear Him being inappropriate. Whatever He touches is often a clue as to what He's looking to heal, redeem, or guide you to. Whatever He says to you will be words that invite you deeper into relationship and transformation. Allow yourself to linger at this moment. Are there songs that you can hear or smells that capture your attention? If there is peace, then ground yourself in that place and allow His peace to permeate your entire being. If there is joy, then allow His joy to come up from deep within you. Maybe there's grief; then, maybe allow Him to bring you deep comfort.

Using your imagination like this in prayer will open up whole conversations with Jesus. He will show you things that you hadn't even hoped, dreamed, or dared to imagine. The more you do this the more familiar you become with what the Father's speaking to you. It's like working a muscle, it might be awkward at first, but the more you do it the stronger it will become.

Take the time to write down what you see and allow this vision to build over time. Next time you come back to the throne room, you

may see different things or people. Jesus may reach out to you differently or say something you have not heard before. I've always found that everything He says has such weight and value for my life in those moments.

His Kingdom is here and you've just encountered it.

LET THERE BE LIGHT

To finish, let's go back to where we started, in Lebanon. There was a day in Lebanon when we travelled out to the border with Syria. This area has historically been a hotspot for hostilities between the Syrians and the Lebanese. Anyone we spoke to in this area had a story of loss, trauma, and grief. Most of the buildings were littered with bullet holes from generations of fighting. These buildings held their own stories.

We were going to observe the work a church in the region was doing with Syrian refugees. This town was a gateway for the Syrian refugees. The Lebanese government wouldn't let them live in anything permanent. So regardless of the season, they lived in a tent city outside the town. In summer, they would swelter and in winter, they would freeze. The church we visited was pioneering care for the refugees, as the Lebanese government refused to provide aid or care. Members of their church were upset that its leadership was doing this and many left the church over it. However, God had sowed a creative seed deep within the heart of this church and by the time we got to see their work, we were watching the harvest happen. They knew what grace looked and felt like. They knew they could not withhold it from these people who were driven from their homeland by war.

This church was daily sending care packages out to the camp. This included basic food and sanitary aid. They had built a school, a laundry, a medical centre, and a community hub. They were building the next phase of it the day we arrived. In walking the site, I found myself remembering our first day in Beirut when we visited a work that was happening in the slums. There was a peace and love present that was tangible. The kids played and we could hear them laugh. They would run up to us, ask us to take their photos, and share with us their hopes and dreams for the future, all the while living in a refugee camp in a country that didn't want them.

While we were there, we began talking with one of the builders through a translator. Most people this far into Lebanon didn't speak English, so every conversation was through a translator. I asked him why he was doing this work. It was a question that puzzled and confused him. I thought the translator must have been asking why he was a builder, and not why was he doing this work for the Syrians. Eventually, we cleared up any misunderstanding and he simply said, "This is not a question that I even ask, it's a work for people that I love."

I stood there dumbfounded by his response. He had every reason to have this question going through his mind and not love these people for what they had generationally done to him and his family. He had personally witnessed the horrifying effects of the Syrians invading his land. But here he was with grace powerfully flowing through every nail he hammered to give the Syrians a safe place to gather. It wasn't even a question in his mind, it was an act of love that changed communities one nail at a time. This man stood on no pedestal or platform. He simply stood with a hammer in his hand and a heart that was wired to love simply and powerfully.

After this moment, I took the time to gather myself and look around. The camp even had a well which they had dug for people. We were there in summer and it was hot. The land was dry and brown. There wasn't much life surrounding this tent city, except for the work that this church was doing. They had water to drink, to wash with, and to water the ground. From the ground, beautiful and lush green grass was growing. It looked so out of place, but here in their midst, life was flourishing. I was looking at a piece of Eden where the people of this church were bringing the love of God and the presence of His Kingdom to earth.

God spoke, "Let there be light..." and saw that it was good. I stood there amid a contradiction, witnessing creation happen through love. It was not even a question.

I do not doubt that God saw this as good and that His hands were all over this. But He did not do this on His own, He invited His people into the conversation of creation. The pastor of this church had felt the draw of God's Spirit to do something with the love he was feeling a few years prior. He knew there would be a cost in pioneering this work. He knew many would likely be angry with him and relationships possibly fractured by it. Eden beckoned for him to walk with God just like Adam and Eve did.

I have taught the love, grace, and forgiveness of God for many years. But this one trip into Lebanon changed everything for me. You see, you can teach love, grace, and forgiveness until the day you die and it will remain good teaching, but to experience and encounter these mighty aspects of God's character will transform your life.

It has been two years since I was in Lebanon. There is hardly a day when I don't think of the experiences and encounters I had with God there. It feels like He called me out of hiding and into plain sight there. It feels like so much of what I learned through religion was lifted from me as I witnessed the power of His love at work in a place where I didn't expect it. He opened my eyes to people's journeys and my ears to people's stories. He invited me to see people as He sees them, and what I saw was confronting and glorious. It was confronting because I could see first-hand the suffering and trauma that humankind causes. It was glorious because I was witnessing the supernatural power of love flowing from the hearts of those who choose love without even asking a question about why they should.

I want to leave you with an invitation to live from Eden. Listen again to the experience of God in Genesis 1, "In the beginning God created the heavens and the earth. The earth was formless and empty, and darkness covered the deep waters. And the Spirit of God was hovering over the surface of the waters. Then God said, 'Let there be light,' and there was light." When God speaks, He creates. In John 1:1-5 we read, "In the beginning the Word already existed. The Word was with God, and the Word was God. He existed in the beginning with God. God created everything through him, and nothing was created except through him. The Word gave life to everything that was created, and his life brought light to everyone. The light shines in the darkness, and the darkness can never extinguish it." As God spoke light over the chaos all those years ago, He spoke it from His Son. To listen for His voice is to listen for His Son's. The light that Jesus brought invites us into a relationship, not into a religion. It invites us into freedom, not into obligation. The light reveals the narrow pathway that leads us back into Eden, into the very heart of God. Now nothing separates us from His love and we have permission to enjoy a relationship with Him every day of our lives.

Every story of our life is added to Jesus' Kingdom story. We can see through our stories His deep desire to walk through life with us. His love and grace can be your story as well. As He lives with you, so you live with Him every day.

In our current world of chaos, His Word still creates safety and re-lationship as we dig deeper into The Father. Can you recognise His provision, restoration, and freedom through love in your life? Can you accept His invitation to live from your original design and walk in the Garden with Him every day? This is who we are created to be.

EPILOGUE

I watched as the Designer climbed out of the tree and walked along His familiar paths. I knew that He knew where they were, but He walked as if He didn't. He knew all that they had done. He'd watched every moment unfold, yet He was unhurried. It was the cool of the evening and He so loved walking with them both.

As I sat and watched, I just cried. I cried for the choices that were made, for the effect that this choice had on the entire Garden. I cried for the man and the woman... they now saw things and knew things they wished they hadn't. But most of all, I cried for the Designer. He'd put His best into everything that I could see. Every tree, flower, fruit, mountain, lake, and ocean just leaked His glory. It was just so good!

The confusion in my spirit was real and the feelings I was sensing were impossible to understand and comprehend. As I cried I became aware of another presence beside me; Wisdom sat with me. She was everything that I was, but she carried something more that I needed to hear. I could feel the hope she carried and I wondered whether it would be a hope that would soothe my aching heart.

She turned to me and asked, "Why are you crying?" I nearly fell out of the tree! I couldn't believe that Wisdom was so unaffected by all that had just happened. She just smiled and said, "Oh, you think that this is the end?" I just sat and wept and nodded my head. I couldn't see another outcome. So Wisdom went on, "Did not the Designer tell you that this was the start of the greatest love story ever?" Again, through my tears, I nodded. I'd heard what the Designer said, but I didn't understand Him. Again she smiled and said, "In many years' time One will come and you will see the love song in all of its glory. What makes no sense now will make perfect sense then. This One will talk about a seed. He will explain for new life to happen, a seed needs to die in the ground. Once it has been in the ground for long enough, you will see so much life that this Garden will not be able to contain it. Eagle, can you now see the seed that I speak of?"

"But when will this happen?" I was pleading now. My heart was broken and all I could feel was loss. I couldn't see what Wisdom saw and I couldn't comprehend what she was saying. Once again, Wisdom looked at me and smiled and said, "Eagle, you have been so faithful and you have clung to every word that has been spoken. You know the Designer's words are life and you have felt life flow through you every time He speaks. This is now a time to listen again and to discover again the life force that flows from His words. It is hard, I know, but that does not mean it's impossible. Just listen and hear the Designer's words again."

So my gaze moved then to the Garden, and I heard the Designer calling to the man and the woman. He was calling them by name,

"Adam," "Eve," "Where are you?" It was then that I realized what Wisdom meant! I could hear the words, but it was what I felt that impacted me! I could feel such extraordinary love. Each word was an invitation to heal and not to hide. Each word was a call to restoration and not destruction. Each word was shifting the atmosphere of the Garden again. I could feel life flowing through it again! I could feel order come back again. My soul was soaring and I wanted to take flight and rejoice!

But this time it was Wisdom that reached out and stopped me. I was confused, because I wanted to fly and declare freedom. Wisdom, though, took hold of me and looked in my eyes, and said, "Watch and listen."

So, I watched and as I did, I felt the tears start flowing again. The man and woman weren't feeling the life and love that I was feeling. There was something else at play here. I had felt this same thing when that strange lizard started lurking under the *Tree of Knowledge of Good and Evil*. I started screaming for the Designer to tread on the head of the lizard! Again, I wanted to fly down and destroy that strange lizard.

Wisdom once again held me back and said, "It's not the Designer's responsibility to silence the voice of the lizard. For this to be a love story, Adam and Eve need to choose the Designer's voice above all others." "But Wisdom," I screamed, "They haven't chosen to do that! They're still listening to the lizard!"

Wisdom simply nodded and said, "Yes, but it will not always be so. For now, they will leave this Garden and they will find a new home, and that strange lizard will find out the weight of Eve's heel. But rest assured the Designer will not leave them, and you will again be charged to watch over them. You will see many things; some will burden you and some will make you rejoice. The Garden will close for a time, but it will only be for a time. Remember, the seed needs to die before the new life begins."

As stated at the start of the book, this final chapter, like the first, are simply an allegory of all that you have read within the chapters of this book. I trust that it has been helpful, and who knows, maybe the eagle will be back in the next book!

We are so blessed to publish Matt's first book, and look forward to many more!

The purpose of Truly Loved Media is to continually redirect attention to God, His Word, and His amazing love; to support believers in their faith; to impart truth in a creative way that brings greater revelation and worship to God; to encourage peace for believers with reminders of God's love and promises; and to declare God's Word to pre-believers in such a way that they have a deeper understanding of His love for them.

To read more about our vision
and what we offer, visit us at
trulyloved.media

ABOUT THE AUTHOR

Matt Beckenham

Matt is a pioneer of prophetic expression in the Kingdom. His lens of love stretches beyond the four walls of the church and has ignited a divine rewrite of the narrative of the way Kingdom relationships move and unfold.

Matt, along with his wife, Trish, founded Greater Things International, a safe space for those who are seeking to hear from God. Drawing on their 30 years in ministry and counselling, they are committed to seeing people walk in the freedom of their original design.

Matt's heart is that each of us would sit at the feast table laid out before us by the King of kings, and that we would partake wholly in the riches of being with the Designer as He designed us to be. Matt carries love as a mantle for the remnant. This flows through *Eden's Blueprint* and his work at Greater Things International.

Matt was born in Australia and has always lived there. He's married to Trish and has three adult children. Before stepping into Greater Things International, he was in pastoral ministry for 19 years. Prior to this, he worked in structural and civil engineering as a draftsperson and IT Manager. If he and Trish are not in Sydney, you'll often find them exploring New Zealand, a place that has captured their hearts.

To be a part of this movement, you can find Matt at
greaterthingsinternational.com

Printed in Great Britain
by Amazon